PRINCIPAL
PRODUCTS
OF
PORTUGAL

SOME BOOKS BY DONALD HALL

Essays:

Seasons at Eagle Pond

Their Ancient Glittering Eyes

Life Work

Principal Products of Portugal

Poetry:

The One Day

Old and New Poems

The Museum of Clear Ideas

The Old Life

Children's Books:

Ox-Cart Man

I Am the Dog, I Am the Cat

The Farm Summer 1942

Lucy's Christmas

Lucy's Summer

When Willard Met Babe Ruth

PRINCIPAL PRODUCTS OF PORTUGAL

PROSE PIECES

DONALD HALL

BEACON PRESS · BOSTON

BEACON PRESS
25 Beacon Street
Boston, Massachusetts 02108-2892

Beacon Press books
are published under the auspices of
the Unitarian Universalist Association of Congregations.

99 98 97 96   8 7 6 5 4 3 2

Text design by Christine Raquepaw
Composition by Wilsted & Taylor

Library of Congress Cataloging-in-Publication Data

Hall, Donald, 1928–
Principal products of Portugal: prose pieces / Donald Hall.
p.   cm.
ISBN 0-8070-6202-2 (cloth)
ISBN 0-8070-6203-0 (paper)
I. Title.
PS3515.A3152P75   1995
814′.54—dc20   94-33667

FOR DON CLARK

CONTENTS

CONTENTS

CREDITS

"Art for Life for Art," by Donald Hall, reprinted by permission of the *Dartmouth Alumni Magazine*.

"Auerbach in Bronze," originally published as "Red Auerbach," by Donald Hall, reprinted by permission of *SPORT Magazine*.

"Ballad of the Republic," originally published as "Summer Reading in Mudville, Hope Springs Eternal: Mighty Casey's 100th Season," by Donald Hall, copyright 1988 by The New York Times Company, reprinted by permission; also appeared as the afterword to the centennial edition of *Casey at the Bat* (Boston: Godine, 1988), reprinted by permission.

"Bluejeans and Robert Francis," by Donald Hall, reprinted by permission of *Yankee Magazine*; "The Base Stealer" and "Hide-and-Seek," reprinted from *The Orb Weaver*, by Robert Francis (Wesleyan University Press), copyright 1960 by Robert Francis, reprinted by permission of the University Press of New England; "Good Night Near Christmas" and "Nothing Is Far," reprinted from *Robert Francis: Collected Poems, 1936–1976* (Amherst: University of Massachusetts Press, 1976), copy-

PREFACE

With modesty's familiar flamboyance, in a bravado of self-abnegation, in megalomaniacal diffidence, with exhibitionistic reticence—I call this collection *Principal Products of Portugal*: code for things miscellaneous, unrelated, boring, and probably educational. The title should please not only for its prodigious procession of p's but for its metrical Longfellowship, bringing back memories of *"This* is the *for*est prim*e*val, the *mur-"*—and rote recitation standing in the third grade doing the multiplication tables, 7s maybe, or maybe the principal products of Portugal.

Textiles are big, it appears, and textiles manipulated into clothing; liquor; fruit and vegetables; wood and cork; wood and work manipulated into furniture; fish; pulp and waste paper; pearls and semiprecious stones.

Thus does the writer of essays, gathering a book out of products neither Portuguese nor principal, assemble himself by a title. Doubtless the manufactures of Eagle Pond are baseball, poetry, artists and writers named Henry, basketball, trees, politics, reading, graveyards, art, and Eagle Pond. The author is wary about comparing his work to waste paper, on the one hand, or to pearls, on the other. Semiprecious stones? Maybe, on occasion, he makes something that resembles garnet or tourmaline.

D. H.

BALLAD OF THE REPUBLIC

Somewhere the sun is shining, and somewhere children shout, and somewhere someone is writing, "Casey at One Hundred." A century ago, on June 3, 1888, a twenty-five-year-old Harvard graduate, one-poem poet Ernest Lawrence Thayer, published "Casey at the Bat" in the pages of the San Francisco *Examiner*. I suppose it's the most popular poem in our country's history, if not exactly in its literature. Martin Gardner collected twenty-five sequels and parodies to print in his prodigy of scholarship, *The Annotated Casey at the Bat* (1967; rev. 1984). Will the next Casey bat clean-up in a St. Petersburg Over-Ninety Softball League? Perhaps, instead, we will hear of a transparent Casey on an Elysian diamond, shade swinging the shadow of a bat while wraith pitcher uncoils phantom ball. Or spheroid, I should say.

The author of this people's poem was raised in Worcester, Massachusetts: gentleman and scholar, son of a mill owner. At Harvard he combined scholastic and social eminence, not always feasible on the banks of the Charles. A bright student of

William James in philosophy, he graduated Magna Cum Laude and delivered the Ivy Oration at graduation. On the other hand, he was editor of the *Lampoon*, for which traditional requirements are more social than literary; he belonged to Fly, a club of decent majesty. It is perhaps not coincidence, considering Victorian Boston's social prejudices, that Thayer's vainglorious mock hero carries an Irish name.

After his lofty graduation, Thayer drifted about in Europe. One of his Harvard acquaintances had been young William Randolph Hearst, business manager of the *Lampoon*, expelled from Harvard for various pranks while Thayer was pulling a Magna. The disgraced young Hearst was rewarded by his father with editorship of the San Francisco *Examiner*, where he offered Thayer work as humorous columnist. By the time "Casey" appeared, Thayer had left California to return to Worcester, where he later managed a mill for his father and studied philosophy in his spare time.

He received five dollars for "Casey" and never claimed reward for its hundreds of further printings. By all accounts, "Casey"'s author found his notoriety problematic. As with all famous nineteenth-century recitation pieces—"The Night Before Christmas," "Backward Turn Backward O Time in Thy Flight"—other poets claimed authorship, which annoyed Thayer first because he *did* write it and second because he wasn't especially proud of it. There was the additional annoyance that old ballplayers continually asserted themselves the *original* Casey of the ballad: Thayer insisted that he made the poem up. The author of "Casey at the Bat" died in Santa Barbara in 1940 without ever doing another notable thing.

The poem's biography is richer than the poet's: At first "Casey" blushed unseen, wasting its sweetness on the desert air, until an accident blossomed it into eminence. In New York De Wolf Hopper, a young star of comic opera, was acting in *Prince Methusalem*. On August 15, 1888, management invited players from the New York Giants and the Chicago White Stockings to attend a performance, and Hopper gave thought to finding a special bit that he might perform in the ballplayers' honor. His friend the novelist Archibald Clavering Gunter, recently returned from San Francisco, showed him a clipping from the San Francisco *Examiner*.

In Hopper's autobiography, he noted that when he "dropped my voice to B-flat, below low C, at 'the multitude was awed,' I remember seeing Buck Ewing's gallant mustachios give a single nervous twitch." Apparently Hopper's recitation left everyone in the house twitching for joy, and not only the Giants' hirsute catcher. For the rest of his life, Hopper repeated his performance by demand, no matter what part he sang or played, doomed to recite the poem (five minutes and forty seconds) an estimated ten thousand times before his death in 1935. As word spread from Broadway, the poem was reprinted in newspapers across the country, clipped out, memorized, and performed for the millions who would never hear De Wolf Hopper. Eventually the ballad was set to music, made into silent movies, and animated into cartoons; radio broadcast it, there were recordings by Hopper and others, and William Schuman wrote an opera called *The Mighty Casey* (premiere 1953).

When he first recited the poem Hopper had no notion who had written it. Thayer had signed it "Phin.," abbreviating his college nickname "Phinny." Editors reprinted the poem anonymously or made up a reasonable name. When Hopper played Worcester early in the 1890s, he met the retiring Thayer—and poet recited poem for actor, as Hopper later reported, without a trace of elocutionary ability.

There are things in any society that *we always knew*. We do not remember when we first heard about Groundhog Day, or the rhyme that reminds us "thirty days hath September." Who remembers first hearing "Casey at the Bat"? Although I cannot remember my original exposure, I remember many splendid renditions from early in my life by the great ham actor of my childhood. My New Hampshire grandfather Wesley Wells was locally renowned for his powers of recitation—for speaking pieces, as we called it. He farmed bad soil in central New Hampshire: eight Holsteins, fifty sheep, a hundred chickens. In the tie-up for milking, morning and night, he leaned his bald head into warm Holstein ribs and recited poems with me as audience; he kept time as his hands pulled blue milk from long teats. When he got to the best part, he let go the nozzles, leaned back in his milking chair, spread his arms wide and opened his mouth in a great O, the taught gestures of elocution. He spellbound me as he set out the lines on warm cowy air: "But there is no joy in Mudville—mighty Casey has struck out!" The old barn (with its whitewash over rough boards, with its spiderwebs and straw, with its patched harness and homemade ladders and pitchforks shiny from decades of hand-labor) paused in its shadowy hugeness and applauded again the ringing failure of the hero.

If he had not recited it for me lately, I reminded him. He recited a hundred other poems also, a few from Whittier and Longfellow but mostly poems from newspapers by poets without names. I don't suppose he knew "Ernest Lawrence Thayer" or the history of the poem, but "Casey" itself was as solid as the rocks in his pasture. The word that left Broadway and traveled was: *This poem is good to say out loud.* Earlier, the same news had brought intelligence of Edgar Allan Poe's "The Raven" and Bret Harte's "The Heathen Chinee." Public schooling once consisted largely of group memorization and recitation. The New England Primer taught theology and the alphabet together: "In Adam's fall / We sinned all" through "Zacchaeus he / Did climb a tree / His Lord to see." Less obviously the Primer instilled pleasures of rhyme and oral performance. When we decided fifty and sixty years ago that rote memorization was bad teaching, we threw out not only the multiplication table but also "Barbara Frietchie." Recitation of verse was turned over to experts.

Earlier, for two hundred years at least, recitation and performance took center stage in the one-room schools; but it did not end there. In the schools, recitation-as-performance—not merely memorization to retain information—climbed toward competitive speaking, elimination and reward on Prize Speaking Day, when the athletes of elocution recited in contest before judges. The same athletes did not stop when school stopped, and recitation exfoliated into the adult world as a major form of entertainment. Hamlets and cities alike formed clubs that met weekly for mutual entertainment and variously included singing, playing the violin or the piano, recitation, and political debate. In the country towns and villages, which couldn't afford to hire Mr. Hopper to entertain them (nor earlier Mr. Emerson to instruct and inspire them), citizens made their own Lyceums and Chautauquas. In my grandfather's South Danbury, New Hampshire, young people founded the South Danbury Debating and Oratorical Society. Twice a month they met for programs that began with musical offerings and recitations, paused for coffee and doughnuts, and concluded with a political debate, like: "Resolved: That the United States should Cease from Territorial Expansion."

While recitation thrived, the recitable poem became a way of entertaining ideas and each other, of exposing or exercising public concerns. Poetry in the United States was briefly a public art. But after the Great War came cars, radios, and John Dewey; recitation departed, and poets have been blamed, ever since, for losing their audience. The blame is unfair, because the connection between poetry and a mass audience was brief, nor did it work for all poetry. John Donne never had a great audience; neither did George Herbert nor Andrew Marvell, nor in America Walt Whitman or Emily Dickinson. These poets made poems with a fineness of language that required sophisticated reading, and from most readers silent reading not to mention rereading.

All the same, *some* nineteenth-century poets wrote poems both popular and fine—without being as popular as baseball or as fine as Gerard Manley Hopkins. This moment was the fragile age of elocution. Some poets wrote variously—turning in one direction to talk to the people, and in another to talk to the ages.

Longfellow's best work—the *Divine Comedy* sonnets, "The Jewish Cemetery at Newport"—is dense, sophisticated, adult poetry of the second order. But in his nationalist fervor he also wrote epics of the Republic's prehistory like *Evangeline*, or lyrics of the common life like "The Village Blacksmith." Making these poems, he made recitation pieces; without intending to, he wrote poems for children and for entertainment. When Whittier made "Barbara Frietchie" in his abolitionist passion, he made willy-nilly a patriotic poem to recite in schools. Meantime Walt Whitman—who had notions about poetry for the people— went relatively unread as he went largely unrecited. Mind you, he showed he could turn his hand to the recitation piece: "O Captain My Captain" is poetically inferior to "Casey."

The twin phenomena of recitation and the popular poem thrived in England at the same time, and Macaulay's *The Lays of Ancient Rome* turned up in American school readers and on Prize Speaking Days. The public Tennyson, laureate not melancholic, wrote verses often memorized for performance; lyrical Wordsworth and bouncy Browning served as well. There were many English sources, even for "Casey at the Bat": Thayer remembered looking into W. S. Gilbert's *Bab Ballads* before composing "Casey."

At my grammar school in the 1930s we memorized American poets: "O Captain My Captain" for Whitman, Joaquin Miller's "Columbus," something by James Whitcomb Riley. The trajectory of the recitation piece, of which "Casey" is a late honorable example, began its descent early. James Whitcomb Riley scored hits with "Little Orphant Annie" and others, but Riley was mostly hokum. Then there was Eugene Field, whose "Little Boy Blue" is gross sentimentality accomplished with skill; then there is Ella Wheeler Wilcox; then there is Edgar Guest. (The Canadian Robert Service is a late recitable anomaly.) Vachel Lindsay and Carl Sandburg were themselves performers who seldom gave rise to performance in others; they led from recitation toward the poetry reading. There are poets today as sentimental and popular as Edgar Guest but they write free verse and no one recites them.

The tradition of recitation survives only in backwaters, like Danbury, New Hampshire. If you come to our elementary school on Prize Speaking Day and sit in the school cafeteria-gymnasium-auditorium, a miniature elocutionist may break your heart reciting "Little Boy Blue," or you may watch a stout ten-year-old outfielder, straight out of central casting, begin: "The outlook wasn't brilliant for the Mudville nine that day . . ."

Among the thousands of pieces memorized and recited, in the Age of Elocution, few survive. Why "Casey at the Bat"? For a hundred years this mock heroic ballad has lurked alive at the edges of American consciousness. It has endured past the culture that spawned it. When an artifact like this clownish old poem persists for a century, surviving not only its moment but its natural elocutionary habitat, there must be reasons. There must be public reasons for public endurance.

We might as well ask: Why has baseball survived? Neither the Black Sox scandal nor the crash nor two world wars nor the

National Football League have ended the game of baseball. Every year more people buy tickets to sit in wooden seats over a diamond of grass—or in plastic seats over plastic grass, as may be. Doubtless we need to ask: *Has* baseball survived? Casey's game pitted town against town with five thousand neighbors watching. Maybe the descendant of Casey's game is industrial league softball played under the lights by teams wearing rainbow acrylics. These days when we speak of baseball we mostly mean the major leagues, millionaire's hardball, where our box seats place us half a mile from a symmetrical petrochemical field. Do we watch the game that Mudville watched? Yes.

As "Casey at the Bat" survives the culture of recitation, the game's shape and import survive its intimate origins. Not without *change*: If the five thousand ghosts of the Mudville crowd, drinking a Mississippi of blood to turn solid, as in Homer's day, reconstituted themselves on a Friday night at Three Rivers Stadium to witness combat between Cincinnati's team and Pittsburgh's, they would gape in spiritual astonishment at the zircon-light of a distant diamond under velvet darkness, at the pool-table green of imitation grass, at amenities of Lite, at the wave, at the skin color of many players, at tight uniforms, and at a scoreboard that showed moving pictures of what just happened.

But in their ectoplasmic witness they would also observe the template of an unaltered game. They would watch a third baseman move to his left, stopping the ball with his chest, picking the ball up to throw the runner out; or a second baseman flipping underhand to a shortstop pivoting toward first for the double play, or an outfielder charging a line drive while setting himself to throw. Above all, they would see a pitcher facing a batter late in the game with men on base. They would see a clean-up man approaching the batter's box with defiance curling his lip. "Casey at the Bat" survives—to begin with—because it crystallizes baseball's moment, the medallion carved at the center of the game, where pitcher and batter confront each other.

There are other reasons, literary and historical. When a poem is so popular, one needs to quote Mallarmé again, and observe that poems are made of words. "Casey"'s language is a small consistent comic triumph of irony. The diction is mock heroic, big words for small occasions: When a few fans go home in the ninth inning, they depart not in discouragement or disdain but "in deep despair." The remaining five thousand require a learned allusion: In his *Essay on Man*, Alexander Pope wrote that, "Hope springs eternal in the human breast," and Thayer of course knew the source of his saw; but Pope, like Shakespeare, is largely composed of book titles and proverbs: Thayer uses Pope not as literary allusion but as appeal to common knowledge by way of common elevated sentiment.

Elevation is fundamental: Despite the flicker of hope, the crowd is a "grim multitude"—language appropriate to Milton's hell—and if the hero is mocked, hero-worshipers are twice mocked. Thayer's poetic similes are Homeric—as if Achilles faced Hector instead of Casey the pitcher. (If Casey is not quite Achilles, at least he is Ajax.) Imagery of noise, loud in Homer and his echo Virgil, rouses Thayer to exalted moments: A yell "rumbled through the valley, it rattled in the dell; / It knocked upon the mountain and recoiled upon the flat." This yell is cousin to the "roar / Like the beating of the stormwaves on a stern and distant shore." It is noise again when Thayer's crowd reacts to a called strike: " 'Fraud!' cried the maddened thousands, and echo answered fraud." These days at Fenway Park the bleacherites divide themselves for a rhythmic double chant, but they do not say "Fraud." When they feel polite they cry "Less filling" and echo answers "Tastes great."

Possibly crowds were not chanting "Fraud" in the 1880s either. It was a major form of Victorian humor to elevate diction over circumstance. Mr. Micawber soared into periphrastic euphemism to admit that he was in debt; W. C. Fields was an orotund low-comedy grandson. For a hundred years it was witty or amusing to call kissing osculation, and to refer to a house as a domicile. If somebody missed our tone, we sounded pompous, but usually people understood us: When we enjoyed something common or vulgar (like baseball) we could show a humorous affection for it, yet retain our superiority, by calling the ball a spheroid.

This habit of language has not entirely disappeared, but more and more it looks like an anglophile or academic *tic*. The late poet and renowned advocate of baseball, Marianne Moore, always talked this way, never more than when she spoke of the game. When she identified the Giants' pitcher, "Mr. Mathewson," we are told that she noted: "I've read his instructive book on the art of pitching, and it's a pleasure to note how unerringly his execution supports his theories." Another St. Louis poet was T. S. Eliot, born the same year as "Casey," and like Moore expert in the humor of a polysyllabic synonym for a homely word. Eliot is the most eminent poet influenced by "Casey at the Bat." *Old Possum's Book of Practical Cats* includes "Growltiger's Last Stand," conflation of Custer and Casey, written in metrical homage and in allusion: "Oh there was joy in Wapping when the news flew through the land." Growltiger is a vicious fellow, racist or at least nationalist ("But most to Cats of foreign race his hatred has been vowed"), and loathed by felines of an Asian provenance. Absorbed in romantic adventure he is surrounded by a "fierce Mongolian horde," captured, and made to walk the plank.

The author of *Four Quartets* and "The Love Song of J. Alfred Prufrock" grew up in the age of recitation; we could be certain that he knew "Casey" even if "Growltiger" were not written in homage. Like many poets he could write high or low, wide or narrow; unlike some poets, when he wrote for children he recognized that he was doing it.

Mockery is "Casey" 's point, with humor to soften the blow. After the crowd (which is us), the great Casey himself takes the brunt of our laughter. His name is the poem's mantra, repeated twenty-two times, often twice in a line: As he puffs with vainglory, "Defiance gleamed in Casey's eye, a sneer curled Casey's lip." The hero's role is written in the script of gesture. After five stanzas of requisite exposition, we catch sight of the rumored Casey in the sixth stanza: "There was ease in Casey's manner." By this phrase we are captured and the double-naming locks us in: "There was pride in Casey's bearing and a smile on Casey's face." We know the smile's message, and we know how Casey doffs his cap. Casey is Christlike: It is "With a smile of Christian charity" that he "stilled the rising tumult"; if we remember that this metaphoric storm occurs at sea ("the beating of the stormwaves"), we may understand that Casey's charity earns its adjective.

And every time we hear "Casey at the Bat," the hero strikes out. We require this failure.

Not all of us. My grandfather with his sanguine temperament always regretted that Casey struck out. He memorized the sequels and tried them all, especially "The Volunteer." In Clarence P. MacDonald's poem, printed in the San Francisco *Examiner* in 1908, the home team plays with no bench; behind in the game, it loses its catcher to an injury, and the captain calls for a substitute from the stands: A grayheaded volunteer finishes the game as catcher and his home run wins the game in the ninth. Besieged by teammates and fans to reveal his identity, the weeping stranger proclaims: "I'm mighty Casey who struck out just twenty years ago."

Wonderful.

But it won't do. None of the triumphant sequels will do. None show the flair of Thayer's ballad, its vigorous bumpety heptameter and mostly well-earned rhymes, or its consistently overplayed language. Most important, none celebrates failure: Casey must strike out: Casey's failure is the poem's success.

When Thayer first published "Casey at the Bat" in 1888, it

bore a subtitle seldom reprinted: "A Ballad of the Republic."
Once we lived in heroic times: once—and then again. When we
suffer wars and undertake explorations we require heroes, and
Jeb Stuart must gallop behind Union lines, Lindbergh fly the At-
lantic, Davey Crockett enter the wilderness alone, Washington
endure Valley Forge, the Merrimack attack the Monitor, Neil
Armstrong step on the moon, and U. S. stand for Ulysses S.,
Unconditional Surrender, *and* the United States.

The Civil War, which ripped the country apart, began the
work of stitching it together again. (One small agent of integrity
was baseball, as blue and gray troops played the game at rest and
even in prison camps, even North against South as legend tells
us.) For five years North and South lived through the triumphs
and disaster of heroes. Although nameless boys charged stone
walls blazing with rifle fire, we concentrated our attention on
heroic leaders, from dandified cavalrymen to dignified generals.
Sons born to veterans, late in the sixties and early in the sev-
enties, were christened Forrest, Jackson, Sherman, Grant, Lee,
Bedford, Beauregard . . .

But hero-worship is dangerous and needs correction, especially in a democracy if we will remain democratic. To survive
hero-worship we mock our heroes; if we don't we become their
victims. Odysseus came home to slay the suitors; Ulysses S. allowed them to fatten on our larder: Heroic governance became
disaster as the triumphant general turned into the ruinous president. Many other heroes struck out. When the romantic vainglorious George Custer, with his shoulder-length hair, made
combat with Geronimo in 1876, Growltiger walked the plank.

Affluence and corruption, defeat and corruption bred irony. Violence of reconstruction and violence of antireconstruction eventually encouraged detachment from crowd passion.

Whatever young Thayer had in mind, writing his "Ballad of the Republic," 1888 was a presidential year. We elected the mighty Benjamin Harrison president, a former officer of the Union Army, who took the job in a deal and installed as secretary of state the notorious James G. Blaine. De Tocqueville stands behind this poem as much as Homer does. Democracies choose figures to vote in and out of office—to argue over, to ridicule: We do not want gods or kings—that's why we crossed the ocean west—but human beings, fallible like us.

We pretend to forgive failure; really we celebrate it. Bonehead Merkle lives forever and Bill Maserowski's home run diminishes in memory. We fail, we all fail, we fail all our lives. The best hitters fail, two out of three at-bats. If from time to time we succeed, our success is only a prelude to further failure— and success's light makes failure darker still. Triumph's pleasures are intense but brief; failure remains with us forever, a featherbed, a mothering nurturing common humanity. With Casey we all strike out. Although Bill Buckner won a thousand games with his line drives and brilliant fielding, he will endure in our memories in the ninth inning of the sixth game of the World Series, one out to go, as the ball inexplicably, ineluctably, and eternally rolls between his legs.

TREES

The hurricane of 1938 uprooted a forest of rockmaple high on Ragged Mountain—chopping-block trees that lie unrotted still, horizontal, as hard as crowbars. Or they lie so in my mind. On the unimagined Ragged, I trudge every day up New Canada Road with the dog, looking at trees as they tell seasons, decades, and lifetimes.

Mountains are volatile enough: Ferns come and go, streams flood or trickle or dry up; but mountains are adamant also. Granite stays the same; stones please by their stillness and inability to compromise; stones never lie or bomb Baghdad. We envy them for being what we aren't. They are not kin; traveling just so far into stones, we meet a hard boundary: That fellow is still trying to teach one to talk.

On the other hand, trees as they change change slowly. The tree is the rock that changes and the fern that endures. I walk among woods mixed of hard and soft, deciduous and conifer, longlived and brief. Here stands of birch alter like grasses, crazy-barked womanly trees, sometimes thick-waisted and old, mostly slim and wavery like cane, like bamboo, like grass—only *white*. Here the glowering hemlock *Will Not Budge* and pines aspire skyward like eighteenth-century mast-trees.

Relentless station, obdurate return: We envy trees their fixity and their resolute fecundity. Cut the tree down, burn it, blow it over; green commences again. Trees provide for trees by scattering themselves in early summer, sexual seeds lofty in the air; or in autumn the pine trees gliding out aerodynamic cones. I cherish most the spendthrift oak with its small pig-flower acorns dropping from great durable trunks and branches, or little twin testicle-breasts, or green nipples of metallic green bouncing and rolling: squirrelmeat, underfoot ballbearings.

Trees factor autumn and the leaf. Tell it again, how the vanguard swampmaple flame-flowers out late-August, the elegant sumac close behind, then sugarmaple Chinese red, birch yellow, popple pale, until the great oak slow-burns, turning a deep dark russet, filemot or *fleurs mortes* of the remnant joyous dour shades of fallen summer.

Leafless, the trunk stands itself clear, trunk that is tree's stark signature and soul: marker of the dying upright year, durance of gray harsh bark; vertical of stopped upward motion, fixed and permanent principle of tree; organic Stonehenge and Easter Island of winter wood; stark winter totem of imagined summer's leaf and sap.

Or take it forward, how in spring erectile buds engorge at the branch's tip, as evidential as snowdrops and greater in consequence, signal of sun's approach and the relenting year; how edges of pale green uncurl from the natal wrap, loosen, loom, and shake out tentative wild pennants of May—by gesture of leaf restoring green to the upgrowing hill and meadow; and how, in July, the matron-leaf of a hidden male trunk rolls summer's glory out, dark leathery green of the broad fullgrown leaf.

By trees we feed ourselves at the year's table.

Here at the field's edge the beavers harvest their tree-farm, popple the local favorite. Cone-stumps pierce the air. Trunks too long to carry stretch on the ground, warehouses of the practical branch—and the branches are cone-cut. At the edge the beavers' tree-path slips under the railroad fence down which fattails drag household materials all night, up which they climb each night after dark to sharpen teeth at their tree-farm.

Trees are our kind, and kin-trees talk, murmurous and confidential; they rustle or whisper, they tear in brute wind and make almost wordless continuous converse in the regular day. Trees give shape to wind we cannot see; trees make the wind visible and audible: image and song, exhibition and concert, mobile of air and improvised stanza. Trees are clay for the sculptural wind; trees are strings for the virtuoso air; trees are tongues for the tongueless and shapes for blind eyes.

Walking in the woods we listen and watch and feel. Let leaf and needle brush hands, face, or limbs; let the sweet gum of the spruce dribble and shine. We stumble over dead trees that decay full length growing green moss. We straggle among trees that start and struggle, die and prevail. Trees measure hours and years. At the south side of our woodshed a durable oak rises beside a boulder that weighs at least a thousand pounds. The 1938 hurricane blew the tall tree over, roots kicking out of the ground like frozen dancers. My cousin Freeman, who enjoyed a project, winched the oak upright, cabled it to the shed, and with his rock-moving tripod rolled this boulder to press down those roots. The oak stays strong, with its prodigious autumn crop of acorns, holds onto its leaves through winter into cold spring. The strong tree ages, dropping a branch, each August approaching closer to certain and far-off death.

Houses of birds and bears! Mouse-place, coon-domus, mossharbor! Oilwell of maplesyrup, seed factory, leaf gallery, acorn mill! Place holder! Sponsor of rocking chair and fire! Sawdust queen, erect splintery ghost, maiden of pale green newleaf, matron of russet! Ghostwhite of austere bark! Shadowdark woody nation! Sculpture erupted from dirt! New green, old green, new red! Unmitigated slow energy, green in leaf and gray in bark! Handsome erect endurer! Stark winter cross, lithe spring messenger, summer's barque, elegist of autumn!

WORDS OF HENRY ADAMS

The Writer

When he was a young man, Henry Adams made much of his dilemma: He did not know what to *do*. His observations of diplomacy, when he assisted his father at the Court of St. James during the Civil War, prevented him from considering diplomacy as a career. Although he was attracted to science, Harvard's feckless education (as he saw it) left him ill-equipped to follow Agassiz or Lyell. He thought of studying law and emigrating (his metaphor) to St. Louis; but he never followed the thought. Although he spent his life observing and analyzing politics, he felt acute distaste at the notion of running for office—the way his father, grandfather, and great-grandfather had done. As a young man he admired Charles Sumner, assaulted by a South Carolinian barbarian-cavalier on the floor of the Senate, but as he matured his understanding of the pompous and vengeful senator from Massachusetts altered. He admired few officeholders when he was young, and fewer still as he aged—a Coriolanus almost as contemptuous of himself as he was of his fellows.

What, then, should he do? He expressed his dilemma in his

writing, and writing was what he did and what he had to do. This writing took many forms. Of the millions of words he wrote, mostly we read his autobiography, *The Education of Henry Adams* (1906),* with its superb early reminiscence, its ironies about politics and learning, and finally its historical theory which has dated and diminished. Its rival for readers among Adams's books, *Mont-Saint-Michel and Chartres* (1904),* is vivid in its idiosyncratic notions of the Middle Ages, learned and scrupulous and dotty, consumed by an ironic Mariolatry that reminds us of Adams's lifelong devotion to women—at the same time as it qualifies this devotion.

Less often than these works, we read Adams's novels, especially the tart, anonymously issued *Democracy* (1880), which remains not only a pleasing narrative but also a cynical and shrewd analysis of American political mores. (Henry James said of it—not knowing that his friend had written it—that it was well enough done to have been worth doing better.) *Esther* (1884) is less of a novel, but interesting for its light (à clef) on Adams's artistic circle—H. H. Richardson, Saint Gaudens, John La Farge. Too few readers undertake Adams's monumental history of the Jefferson and Madison administrations, which is a major work of American literature. His later essays in historical theory exemplify the misappropriation of ideas and principles from physical science. Adams's last work was a brief biography of the poet George Cabot Lodge, done as a favor to Lodge's family.

The words, the words. When you include the six published

---

*Years of private publication. The books were made public in 1918 and 1913.

volumes of letters, Adams's output is enormous. He was a writer when he claimed that he wasn't. After his wife's early death, he struggled to conclude the history, then renounced authorship and set sail for Asia with John La Farge. On his journey he wrote three or four hours a day, largely letters back home to Elizabeth Cameron.

Henry Adams was a writer by fate, one of our best American writers, and one of our least read. (He is a writer for adults.) Here, I choose to look at portions of his work that are seldom undertaken.

The History

After reading 2,597 pages of Henry Adams's *History of the United States during the Administrations of Jefferson and Madison* (1884–91), I only wish there were 27,000 more. Imagine the tiny dehydrated author, 157 years old in 1995, holed up in Quincy or Beverly Farms, composing his history of later administrations. One hundred and sixty-two pages handle a year, so that somewhere around page 29,000 the diminutive ironist must sketch his account of the latter days of Richard Nixon. He will search for language by which he may do justice to plumbers and bagmen, not to mention their prose styles, not to mention their hairstyles; he will make metaphors for the beat of helicopters hovering over the White House lawn. Heaven knows, when the weary pen finishes describing the famous departure from the White House, we will require it to continue, in tireless democratic outrage, in Roman-Republican ironic tirade, to recount a

Sunday morning pardon, to paraphrase the pieties of the first president from Georgia, to find similes for the strange color of an old man's hair, to contain outrage over the hypocrisies of President Bush's Operation Operation, to . . . No one can imagine what Adamic language will account for allegations about dalliance in Little Rock. But irony will prevail.

Henry Adams's *History* is a monument of our literature. Professional historians have become reticent about attributing literary qualities to history. Witness the dependent clause of a distinguished historian in the *New York Times Book Review*: "Although the Library of America was planned to consist of literary classics, it has already found space for the masterpieces of two historians." For Henry Adams, or for anyone literate a century ago, written history was literature or it was nothing: History was the kind of book that Thucydides, Tacitus, and Gibbon wrote.

Among the genres of literature, history is especially ambitious because it combines study of character, discrimination of probability, moral judgment, and of course imagination. Before Adams undertook this *History*, the American historians Prescott, Bancroft, Parkman, and Motley had already distinguished themselves (Adams was distantly related to Parkman; Adams's wife to Bancroft) and history bulked large in nineteenth-century American literature. Now, ten thousand people have read Melville or Thoreau for every reader of Parkman—and doubtless a hundred thousand for every reader of Henry Adams on the administrations of Jefferson and Madison. Few critics have even pointed us toward this monument. When we teach American literature in college, we teach miniscule poets before we arrive at great historians. Among literary critics only Yvor Winters has recognized and promoted the American historians—very much including the masterwork of Henry Adams. Although one may quarrel about particulars of his judgments (Winters overvalues the melodramatic Motley) one understands again that Winters, in his lifetime routinely ridiculed by everyone who did not canonize him, was righter than almost anybody else.

The best American history is Henry Adams's masterwork, which is also the best work of Henry Adams, better even than the autobiographical chapters of *The Education*. (Only his letters can contest with his *History*.) For the best of the best, one must read the first seven chapters and the last four; these eleven chapters sketch with deft shrewdness the American background at the end of the eighteenth century and the altered nation sixteen years later. These chapters of social history resemble Braudel, with fewer numbers. Adams sets geography against the technologies of transport; we watch an enacted panorama of daily life, accomplished in a scrupulous and expressive prose. The prose is the point. Gibbon began his great work (the first volumes published, fortuitously enough, in 1776) with Gibbonish flair: "In the second century of the Christian AEra, the empire of Rome comprehended the fairest part of the earth, and the most civilized portion of mankind." (This sentence makes my point but I must quote the next: "The frontiers of that extensive monarchy were guarded by ancient renown and disciplined valor." Adjectives owe their unfortunate reputation to bad writers and boring nouns.) Henry Adams, on the other hand, ambitious of contrast and comparison—(he daydreams that we write: "Henry Adams, on the other hand . . . ")—begins amused to make a democratic flatness: "According to the census of 1800, the United States of America contained 5,308,483 persons." Persons! As Yvor Winters remarks, Parkman was the last heroic historian; Adams did something else.

Among the great historians, Henry Adams's *style* does not call attention to itself so much as the styles of Gibbon, Macaulay, and Parkman—not to mention (as I suppose) Tacitus or Thucydides. But it is no glass of water . . . Doubtless some of its relative invisibility derives from its chronological proximity, but its relative plainness speaks for itself: Adams is a democratic (or Republican) stylist, avoiding the dandified and the aristocratic. He is not heroic, except perhaps when he describes war at sea; he avoids the purple passages that glorify and disfigure Parkman; he avoids entirely the fulsome hagiography/demonology of Motley or Macaulay. In his ironic syntax the sentence qualifies when it does not contradict, and the ironist of *The Education* is present in the *History*. In the first half of this *History* Adams's irony is sometimes playful; misanthropy strengthens in the second volume: When someone does a concordance, we will learn that the Imbecility Index multiplied after his wife's suicide.

(Marion Adams, usually known as Clover, killed herself in 1885. The cause of death was generally known and generally kept from print. When James Truslow Adams wrote a biography of Henry, as late as 1930, he could not mention the cause of death; his hints and hesitations, of course, made her death seem lurid. Clover was depressive, and died of her blood chemistry: Her only siblings both killed themselves after she did.)

Adams disparaged the later volumes of his *History* (one must never squint at him quite so hard as when he turns on himself) and he is wrong: Playfulness diminishes; but Adams's fundamental outrage is consistent from beginning to end. The central insight of this *History*, point of departure to which it returns again and again, is a notion that may sound commonplace: *People do the opposite of what they say (and think) they do*. For all his tone of detachment, Henry Adams grabs us by the scruff of the neck, lifts us off the ground, and screams in our ears: People do the opposite of what they say they do! It's true! Everything in the world turns into its own opposite! Doesn't anyone notice?

Heraclitus noticed; Freud noticed.

Adams cannot get over the Jeffersonian paradox: This president, elected to decentralize the federal goverment, centralized it more than any Federalist could have done. When Adams watches Jefferson buy much of the United States, from Napoleon who did not own it, without consulting the people's elected representatives, and put under military rule the new citizens to whom he has promised equal rights, Adams sputters in outrage and astonishment. Of course such reversals are a familiar political phenomenon; it takes Nixon to recognize China. Adams's ironic history records enantiodromia, by which everything becomes its own opposite: Threats of nullification, anticipating secession and the Civil War, almost dissolved the Union at the end of John Adams's unfortunate presidency. For Adams's ironic historical imagination, the screaming point is that it was *New England* that almost seceded over Madison's War of 1812; Fort Sumter almost occurred in Boston Harbor fifty years before Fort Sumter. Maybe a Virginian president would not have sent troops to prevent a United States of New England; in which case, of course, there would have been war anyway.

Adams the New Englander shows continual outrage over the behavior of Massachusetts. If he condescends grossly to the South, he is also profoundly anti-Boston, anti-merchant-class (which was his own class), and anti-Calvinist. A Massachusetts senator named Pickering is far less attractive than Virginians named Jefferson and John Randolph. Although Adams's outrage is general, it is not quite universal; his anger intends to be principled and objective. And Adams's true wrath wholly separates his irony from our contemporary casual semi-intelligent cynicism that dismisses and condescends; habitual irony in the 1990s is a tic, not a vision; based merely on the desire to appear superior, it rises from no moral principle. On the other hand, Adams's outrage—over hypocrisy and double-dealing, over Napoleon's egregious lies, Jefferson's trimming, Aaron Burr's corruption; over evil and imbecility together—reveals under the ironist's mask a true moralist, an old-believer in Democracy.

This anger or even misanthropy is not spread like grape jelly evenly over the historical scene. Some folks are distinctly worse than others—Napoleon, Burr, Burr's sometime accuser General Wilkinson. (Adams is outraged, and almost incredulous, when it turns out that Wilkinson was on a Spanish retainer.) On the other hand, Henry Adams's Jefferson is not wicked but silly, contradictory, hypocritical, Quixotic, absurd, comic, intelligent, and sometimes even endearing. Some of Adams's wittiest passages about Jefferson are fashion notes, describing the president's posture and his embodiment of democratic dress.

On the other hand, some folks are heroic: When Henry Adams describes naval battles in the War of 1812, one hears in the background, as in Cecil B. DeMille, the strains of the national anthem: Adams's generation was brought up on the literature of naval warfare—and Stephen Decatur became a tune for marching to. There are even heroes of politics, diplomacy, and governance. If Adams scorns the illiterate, violent, narcissistic South along with the money-grubbing, hypocritical North, he finds an example of democratic virtue halfway between—in Pennsylvania. Albert Gallatin—responsible, even-headed, honest, judicious—comes close to a model for political man.

My praise never intends to accuse Adams of divine disinterest. An unspoken subplot of this great work must read: "How does an historian handle (on the page and in the psyche) his own family's large part in his subject?" It is common that a descendant, generations removed from the man of action, meditate historically on ancestral behavior—but no occasion rivals this one for eminence of historian combined with family eminence. It has been noted how carefully Adams refrains from speaking of Adams. The historian does not mention his great-grandfather by name for hundreds of pages, a neat trick were it not for the splendor of elegant variation. John Adams is "Washington's successor" as well as "Jefferson's predecessor." John Quincy is not part of the story until the second volume—and his grandson uses him to make Albert Gallatin look better.

It must be acknowledged: In Adams's *History*, not mentioning the name of his great-grandfather—who was president and who favored policies Jefferson first denounced and then employed—roughly resembles hiring a blimp to fly overhead with *John Adams Was My Great-Grandfather* stenciled on its side in letters fifteen feet high.

This great work is *not* unconnected with family and personal history, but the connection is complicated. Henry Adams spent the Civil War in England, a noncombatant helping his father, Ambassador to the Court of St. James, keep the Tories from climbing into the Confederate bed: Observation of Tory hypocrisy left Henry permanently anglophobe. Even in youth, his intelligence would not allow ancestor-worship; but he *admired* his father (not without irony) whose work in the war was diplomacy: And England—rather narrowly, as one gathers—never recognized the Confederacy. For all his objectivity and irony, Adams remains an apologist for his family. Everyone remembers the eloquent, touching pages of *The Education* about the small boy and his grandfather. We sense in these recollections a grandson's protectiveness balming a grandfather's hurt.

All Adamses, Henry not least, considered themselves failures—and for all the achievements of the clan one can understand the notion. Both grandfather and great-grandfather were one-term presidents, first accepted then rejected by their people. (Typically our public men have felt hurt, despised, and rejected—both crooked ones like Nixon and upright ones like Carter.) John Quincy Adams was chosen by the House over Jackson amid allegations of a corrupt deal. Henry Adams felt hurt for the grandfather he knew and loved, and through him for the great-grandfather whose experience oddly resembled his son's. Old John Adams was president of the almost unrecognizable United States described in the first seven chapters of the *History*. John was an austere creature, with a daily life utterly unlike the rich historian's who would be his great-grandchild. John Quincy's America (two thousand pages later) is the prosperous expanding mechanical America de Tocqueville knew and Henry watched as it accelerated toward the twentieth century. John Quincy Adams, in his grandson's eyes, was a Roman Republican governing Nero's Rome.

Henry Adams is no Tory, or not exactly. The real Tories left America sixty years before he was born, leaving Alexander Hamilton and the arch-Federalists as their successors. In American politics and history, the Adamses are an oxymoron, *Democratic* Tories (therefore not Tories) continually glancing back at Roman notions of a Republic headed by noble and reasonable figures of brave probity. This is the heroic and mythic Rome of Livy, not the empire of ironic Tacitus. Adams adds Tacitus' reality to Livy's daydream. Adams watches as the dream disappears into the counting house. He laughs, he sneers, he pokes fun, he is outraged: He is also abashed. He is also filial: The dream would not have vanished so abruptly if his great-grandfather and his grandfather had prevailed.

The Letters

As he wrote the *History*, Henry Adams became a scholar of letters—at least in the form of diplomatic communications. He was more than halfway through his task when Clover died, the catastrophe which turned his remaining decades into continuous anticlimax. Completing the *History* he declared that he was finished as a writer, as his life was finished. For thirty years, this energetic figure called himself posthumous. But as he traveled, or as he resided in Paris or Lafayette Park, he wrote letters half the day. *The Letters of Henry Adams*, six large volumes from Belknap Harvard, provide a selection.

He began the epistolary habit when young. As far back as 1860, during the winter of rebellion, he proposed in a letter to his brother Charles that his correspondence might form a record: "I fairly confess that I want to have a record of this winter on file." At twenty-two he tried out the notion "that a century or two hence when everything else about us is forgotten, my letters might still be read and quoted as a memorial of manners and habits at the time of the great secession." Sixty years later, the old man—being read to by a girl, in Woodrow Wilson's Washington during the Great War—would have mocked the young man who imagined his letters "a memorial."

The words, the words. To read through them—no one may skim these volumes—provides total immersion in the sensibility of an affectionate, irritating, volatile man of ideas and emotions as he reflects on his era and reflects it. Henry Adams has supplied an obsession for American intellectuals in the decades following his death, which means for most of our century. Adams can become a hobby like collecting coins or reading *Finnegans Wake*.

In large part the old snapper is visible in the hatchling. Early he writes, "The world grows, my friend, like a cabbage; or if the simile is vulgar, we'll say, like an oak." His metaphor is organic and comic, rather than mechanical and tragic like his later metaphors. As it continues, the sentence comes to resemble the utterances of his maturity: "the only thing that disgusts me much is the consciousness that we are unable to govern it." His steadiest stance is misanthropy, which achieves provisional wording as early as 1869: "my conceit is not due to admiration of myself but to contempt for everyone else."

The American generation that matured just after mid-century was a generation of genius. In this correspondence, "Harry" is Henry James, younger brother of "Willy." (Harry's letters in four volumes make the *next* best American epistolary collection.) H. H. Richardson is the architect, Oliver Wendell Holmes, Jr. the jurist. These were Harvard associations. Later, John Hay (a Brown man—Lincoln's private secretary and biographer; poet and novelist; ambassador to England; secretary of state) became his closest male friend along with Clarence King (writer and geologist). Adams especially enjoyed acquaintance with visual artists. Besides Richardson, there was John La Farge, with whom he traveled extensively, and other Americans of the moment: We read about dinners with John Singer Sargent; Augustus Saint Gaudens was friend as well as sculptor for Clover's monument in Washington's Rock Creek Cemetery. Later, when Adams summered in Paris and required a wedding present for one of his nieces, he would drop by Rodin's studio to pick something up. Because Adams survived until 1918, his correspondence moves through the generations: We encounter not only George Bancroft, Francis Parkman, Bret Harte, Robert Louis Stevenson, and Curzon, but also Rudyard Kipling, Edith Wharton, Maude Adams, Ethel Barrymore, Bernard Berenson—even Eleanor Roosevelt.

We also meet, alas, Adams's virulent anti-Semitism, about which little can be said unless one attempts a theory of the disease. My metaphor tilts toward the literal. Is it a virus, or a genetic defect, that has afflicted many otherwise intelligent men? In Henry Adams, as later in Ezra Pound, anti-Semitism hardly exists up to a moment in the life—and then like a flashflood it takes over the landscape of character. This anti-Semitism derives from no event; it serves no discernible purpose, economic or otherwise. Where does it come from and what is it for? It is not even accomplished with a sense of malevolence or cruelty. Neither Adams nor Pound *decides* to be anti-Semitic. The singular delusion overtakes them and distorts their thought. It is more like depression or paranoia (of which it partakes) than like robbing banks or kidnapping. The phenomenon is bewildering, and commonplace. For twenty years or more Henry Adams alludes to Jews with hatred, and like Pound gives his obsession an economic provenance in usury. During the Dreyfus affair, Adams's letters make it clear that Dreyfus is guilty although he is innocent—a logical position taken by other conservative or anti-Semitic intellectuals. References to Judaism pour into these letters from angles as loony as Pound's Weinstein Kirchberger. Adams's sister married a Kuhn. Writing an English friend, Adams says that he too has Jewish in-laws, because "Kuhn" is "Cohen." A footnote reveals that Adams's brother-in-law Kuhn was neither Cohen nor Jewish; apparently Adams could make an assumption but could not ask a question. Late in life, his anti-Semitism diminishes virtually to nothing—as if it derived from blood chemistry and altered with hormonal changes.

Outside this bizarre obsession, and despite it, his brain continued to function. The language of this intelligence was epigrammatic and often memorable. Politics was the overrriding subject, and over the years Adams became politically unpredictable—imperialist at one moment and liberal-democrat at another. Unpredictability kept him decent, honest, and unelectable. Insofar as the word means anything, Adams is conservative; but he would have had no truck with the Whiggery of today's neoconservatives. Like a Tory he believes in original sin. "Perfect freedom," Adams writes his English friend Charles Milnes Gaskell:

> becomes the most objectionable form of slavery. I do not know what it is that makes man so base an animal, but true it is that his own good requires him to be bridled and saddled, moderately worked, and his mind carefully filled with details, if he is to be contented. He is not made for unlimited freedom. His mind when it has no daily chopped food set before it, begins to eat itself . . .

Checks and balances start with expulsion from Eden.

In subject matter, these letters touch on everything—with a corrosive, monumental, and irritating intelligence. He is horrified about Armenian genocide, eloquent on numismatics, comical in his ironic "conservative anarchism," fascinated by Egypt and anthropology; in his eighties he stops to wonder why there is so little *weather* in classical literature. In his curiosity and intellectual energy, he starts after every hare. When he was old enough to have difficulty seeing and walking—but kept his hearing—he studied medieval song, with characteristic chutzpah forming his own theories, starting his own musicology if not quite his own composition.

By the time he had finished his youthful European adventure, before the War, he knew that law school was not for him. What to do? Being an Adams was a duty and suggested a direction. "You know I'm ambitious," he writes his mother, "not on my own account, but as a family joint-stock affair." Earlier the direction would have been governance, but Henry's generation stayed aloof from practical politics. Later in life he blamed the corruption and vulgarity of postwar Washington for disempowering him (1911: "I have always considered that Grant wrecked my own life") but the young Adams already leaned toward literature. While earlier Adamses made history as presidents and diplomats, Henry's generation made history in the form of paragraphs—political history that deplored politics and was consumed by it.

The Adams line altered from colonial rough homespun into Henry's raw silk irony. This irony never precluded ambition. At twenty-two Henry writes a brother that he has been reading Gibbon—"Striking, very"—and "after long argument and reflexion I feel much as if perhaps some day I might come to anchor like that." So he did. Young, he would emulate the great historian in service to the Adams family; and the ironical octogenarian proposed to reorder history according to the second law of thermodynamics.

Science, viewed from some distance, was a passion from the start. Adams deplored his inadequate mathematics, blaming it as usual on Harvard College. (He blamed Harvard and Boston for everything he could not blame on Grant.) The first volume of these letters comes largely out of London during the Civil War. If this sojourn provided a shadow Ph.D. in diplomatic history, it allowed him to minor in geology. Reading these letters, we visit the historical adventurousness of the Victorian gentleman scientist, before the players took over. In London he made acquaintance with Sir Charles Lyell, and when he returned to Massachusetts the young man published a massive review of the latest edition of Lyell's *Geology*. When Adams in the 1880s sailed among South Sea archipelagoes, he delighted to criticize a lesser Darwinian theory.

The intelligence of this amateur scientist had room for anxiety, even in its youth. In 1862, he warned with an awful prescience:

> Man has mounted science, and is now run away with. I firmly believe that before many centuries more, science will be master of man. The engines he will have invented will be beyond his strength to control. Some day science may have the existence of mankind in its power, and the human race commit suicide, by blowing up the world.

But, for the young Adams, science was gallant adventure. As he aged, science and technology became obsessions; the Chicago World's Fair of 1893 afflicted him with the dynamo. In the older man, we find the modern humanistic intellectual's familiar poor-cousinship to hard science, misthought by misapplication of rumors of science—as with his late historical theory by which he proproses to apply the idea of entropy to the progress and regress of nations. Historical determinism is a quasireligious determination to find design, "If design govern in a thing so small." Conscious always of decay in the body politic—all of us, aging, find the world aging with us—Adams tried to derive the cooling of our civilization from the cooling of the earth. In 1909 only William James, among Adams's correspondents, spoke a clear negative. In the last year of his life, sick and weak, the old philosopher wrote Adams gruffly from Bad Nauheim: "to tell the truth, it doesn't impress me at all . . . the 'second law' is wholly irrelevant to 'history.'"

In a way, I think that Adams knew it. When Yeats was working out his system, later codified into *A Vision*, he took instruction from his wife's automatic writing. But Yeats was a skeptical man (you can tell he is a skeptic because he seems so gullible) and he tells a story: Once he asked his voices if he should abandon poetry and devote all his time to promulgation of their theories; the voices became agitated and said *No!* After all, they said, we come to give you metaphors for poetry. And Adams wrote, in a letter about history and the second law of thermodynamics, "You will see, because you know our art, that the idea is not what we care most for. We care for the arts with which the architect develops his idea."

Taking sentences here and there from these artful letters, one could put together three hundred pages of extraordinary passages about politics and history. As an older man especially, he writes in continual wrath, with fierce anger at conventionality and at growing old. He loves to say outrageous things: "Athens was always rather a joke, even among the Greeks." Writing Elizabeth Cameron he is witty and serious when he talks about American politics. There are long denunciations of his old student, Senator Henry Cabot Lodge from Massachusetts. We encounter his progressive disillusion with Teddy Roosevelt, whom he liked when Roosevelt was youngish; after Roosevelt became president, T.R.'s vanity and self-absorption came to disgust Adams. "If you remark to him that God is Great, he asks naively at once how that will affect his election." Writing Lucy Baxter earlier, Adams had noticed: "One fool is much like another. So is one President."

Science, history, poetry, politics—and sports. It is startling to hear Henry Adams complain that Harvard has lost football games to Yale in 1891, 1892, 1893, and 1894. It is shocking to discover that Adams is another literary figure attracted to professional baseball, maybe the earliest after Whitman. As early as 1889 he writes to Elizabeth Cameron from Quincy, "Our present occupation here is base-ball. Miss Baxter, my brother John, Dwight and I go in with a covy of brats to see Boston play this, that, and the other club"; to John Hay, "We saw your Cleveland heroes beat our Boston swells, and Chicago get a severe rebuke from us"; and (from the District) "I went to base-ball yesterday and saw the Senators rattle the Bowery Boys, the third game running." The nickname is helpfully footnoted with a lifespan: "The New York Giants, 1883–1957."

Reading these volumes I want to extract sentences to wall-paper rooms with. In 1892 he wrote a brother: "Generally speaking I find the universe as a preposterous fraud, and human beings as fit only for feeding swine; but, when this preliminary understanding is once fully conceded, I see nothing in particular to prevent one from taking a kindly view of one's surroundings." Of course he is an egoist: "Every one of us has to be fired out of a cannon to be roused into consciousness of anything but ourselves." If no cannon lies to hand, addressing a letter may do the trick. As much as he is misanthropic, he shows a genius for friendship. This Timon of Athens loved many people, and the six volumes are crowded with the affectionate gregariousness of this misanthrope. He writes marvelous letters to males—John Hay, Clarence King, Charles Milnes Gaskell, John La Farge, early his brother Charles and late his brother Brooks—but his friendships with women loom larger than his friendships with men.

His love for Clover is clear, although there are few letters because they were seldom apart. (In 1936, Ward Thoron edited *The Letters of Mrs. Henry Adams*, long out of print now. Her letters are witty, intelligent, acerb; when Henry James calls her "Voltaire in petticoats," one understands; as one understands James's praise for her "intellectual grace and moral spontaneity.") It is devastating to follow her presence and absence in these volumes. As everyone notices, Adams did not mention her in his autobiography; by some this void has been taken as a sign of coldness—which is not the first time that the equator has been mistaken for the north pole. Late in life, when he wrote condolences, especially to a male friend who had lost his wife, Adams was heartbreaking in his grief that remained intact after decades.

He loved many other women in many ways. Even before Clover's death, he felt an infatuation for Elizabeth Cameron. Although his grief for Clover remained forever harsh, he came to love Elizabeth Cameron until he died, almost certainly without a love affair. We know a great deal about his love for Cameron because he wrote hundreds of thousands of words to her, doubtless the best of his letters. Some late pages are relaxed, gossipy and funny and passionate—as he does up the politicians of the day—but in the early years after Clover's death, we read fully aware of the tension attendant upon self-denial. In one letter he alludes to a short story about a man, in love with a married woman, who is too circumspect to have an affair. Cameron's husband, a senator without brains or scruples, was nominally Adams's friend. Years of correspondence include passages that read like code; they allude to possible alterations of their relationship. There are calmer years, and then a horror: Patricia O'Toole lets us understand (in *The Five of Hearts*, which details the friendship of the Henry Adamses, the John Hays, and Clarence King—the best book on Adams bar Samuels's biography) how Adams watched while Cameron enjoyed an autumnal affair with the much younger poet Trumbull Stickney.

Adams loved many women, mostly without physical intimacy. In *Mont-Saint-Michel and Chartres*, he entertains himself with Mariolatrous fantasies—and in the letters one glimpses Adams's nympholepsy—a disease which on the whole sponsors benign results in Adams. He writes marvelous letters to nieces, real ones and the courtesy kind—with whimsy when the girls are little, with serious affection and avuncular concern as they grow up. He educated bevies of nieces in his Paris summers. This small starchy figure, as we read through the volumes, turns out to be a Gargantua of affection. (He kept toys in a Washington cupboard to entertain visiting children.) Naturally he was aware of his contrasting manner, his public appearance of stiffness; he could not help himself—but if he had, no one would have noticed. As he once wrote E. L. Godkin, "For twenty-five years, more or less, I have been trying to persuade people that I don't come from Boston and am a heartless trifler. I might as well try to prove that I am an ornithorhyncus of the siluroid civilization." He continues, "If I stood on Fifth Avenue and in a state of obvious inebriety hugged and kissed every pretty woman that passed, they would only say that I was a cold Beacon Street aristocrat."

The *Lodge*

The *Life of George Cabot Lodge* (1911) was the last book Henry Adams wrote. (In 1919 his brother Brooks assembled a posthumous collection, *The Degradation of the Democratic Dogma*.) This biography, unavailable now in facsimile or reprint editions, is most easily found in *The Shock of Recognition*, where Edmund Wilson collected it. It's a small book, much of it perfunctory or dutiful—yet it is worth reading. In this tour of the less-read books of Henry Adams, it provides a conclusion.

"Bay" Lodge wrote four volumes of poetry without committing a memorable poem and died when he was thirty-six. Adams undertook this *Life* at the request of Bay's surviving parents: Henry Cabot Lodge had been a student of Adams's at Harvard and became a senator for whom Adams felt contempt; on the other hand, Adams felt massive affection for the senator's wife, Bay's mother Anna Cabot Mills Davis Lodge. Although Adams was fond of Bay Lodge—apparently an attractive and ebullient man, whom Edith Wharton touchingly recollected in *A Backward Glance*—he shows no illusions about the poems; but he would not refuse the request of the woman he called Sister Anne.

The biography is padded with inconsiderable letters by its subject, and will remind readers of another trifling production by a major writer—the *William Wetmore Story and His Friends* that Henry James wrote at the request (and with the financial support) of the Story family. In one detail the two books differ, for James filled his pages not only by reprinting dull letters but by introducing personal reminiscence. Adams studiously avoids saying "I," even as he provides information clearly out of memory; as a result, Adams appears more egotistical than James. In other respects, these strange books resemble each other: James's *Story*, mostly unreadable, contains superb passages about art and the commitment of the serious artist—Henry James writing about what consumed his life. Adams's *Lodge* includes exegesis of Bay Lodge's failure as a poet; more to the point, if not to the conscious point, it explores the failure of poetry in Adams's New England—and in Adams.

It is not always remarked that Henry Adams's mind was suf-
fused with poetry. Although his prose is a tissue of poetic allu-
sions and paraphrases, this Lodge biography is the only place,
bar his letters, in which Adams speaks about contemporary
verse. Attention to medieval romance, in *Mont-Saint-Michel
and Chartres*, extends to nimble verse translation. But Adams
also wrote his own poems, as surreptitiously as he wrote his
novels. Readers of the Library of America Adams may look into
his "Buddha and Brahma," and his superior "Prayer to the Virgin of Chartres" with its appended "Prayer to the Dynamo."
These poems are thought-ridden (as Adams writes about
Lodge's poems, his commentary always embodies the philosophical heresy) but elsewhere in the letters there are lines of
another order. Henry Adams as poet sometimes does better than
Bay Lodge; he can write a line, turn his heel on a rhyme, and
work out a simile. How close did Adams come to devoting himself to the art of poetry?

Maybe not very close. His familial Bostonian irony impeded
a required poetic devotion. But in his anguish over Clover's
death, twinned by despair over unfulfilled love for a married
woman, he turned privately to the poetry he would not publicly
undertake. On his way into the Pacific with John La Farge, Adams pities himself as he addresses a sonnet called "Eagle Head"
to Elizabeth Cameron. He compares the sea to a heart that "rest-
lessly / Beats against fate, and sobs unceasingly, / Most beautiful flinging itself away, / Clasping the rock by which it must not
stay, / Sublimest in revolt at destiny." His best lines turn up in a
letter to Cameron written at Apia in Samoa and dated "Novem-

ber 25, 1890. 4 o'clock, A.M." (If the poem was not a moment's improvisation, he surely wanted Cameron to think it was.) The poem begins:

> The slow dawn comes at last upon my waking;
> The palms stand clear against the growing light;
> And where long hours I heard the ocean breaking,
> I see at last the broken line of white.

A reader may think of Tennyson's "On the bald street . . ." but a closer influence is Clough. Then Adams becomes familiar, or sentimental, in this poem that remained a private letter ("Martha" is Elizabeth Cameron's child and "Dobbitt" her pet name for Adams):

> I know that, where you are, the noon is falling;
> I look once more down the familiar street;
> Below is Martha for her Dobbitt calling;
> I hear the patter of her eager feet.
>
> John Hay is hurrying from his house to meet us;
> My sister Anne is coming up the stair;
> But still I strain to see the street beneath us,
> To catch the whiteness of the dress you wear.

In the last line begins the poetry, which continues:

> It is the surf upon the coral streaming,
> The white light glimmering on the village lawn;
> The broad banana-leaf reflects the gleaming;
> The shadowy native glides across the dawn.
>
> Death is not hard when once you feel its measure;
> One learns to know that Paradise is gain;
> One bids farewell to all that gave one pleasure;
> One bids farewell to all that gave one pain.

The best of these lines, for all their self-pity, look relatively handsome in this bleak period of American poetry.

But if Adams's best poetry began at 4:00 A.M. on November 25, 1890, apparently it concluded about 4:30 A.M. Commitment to fiction was dangerous to Adams, and to poetry more so. He says that for the Bostonian—Bay Lodge's sort, which is to say his own sort—

> Poetry was a suppressed instinct: and except where, as in Longfellow, it kept the old character of ornament, it became a reaction against society, as in Emerson and the Concord School, or, further away and more roughly, in Walt Whitman. Less and less it appeared, as in earlier ages, the natural, favored expression of society itself. In the last half of the nineteenth century, the poet became everywhere a rebel against his surroundings.

When Adams lists Longfellow and Emerson, he knows that they are second-rate poets compared to the great English; and he cannot quite stomach Walt Whitman. On the other hand, Bay Lodge adored Whitman, "loved him" says Adams "to fanaticism"— without appearing to learn anything from him. Lodge missed Whitman's point, writing poems that still held out supplicating arms only to England—and to a late Victorian England limited in poetic range, a literary culture that saw poems as commendable ideas accompanied by sugary noises; a literary culture that never found room in its poetry—except for the unpublished Hopkins—for the powers of ambivalence and conflict.

Reading Adams on Lodge, one reads more Adams than Lodge. We read much about Lodge's contempt for his potential public, a theme familiar to readers of Adams's letters.

But to feel contempt for one's readers may show too much concern about one's readers. Henry Adams could not imagine a poet *dismissive* of society—the way Eliot, say, looked upon readers of the Boston *Evening Transcript*. The contempt or anger of the old Adams depends upon nostalgia for a relationship to an audience which probably never existed; this contempt resembles his political feelings about the degradation of the democratic dogma. The people elected Adams's great-grandfather president, and again his grandfather—but the newer generations showed no interest in his father, nor in Henry himself. When Adams writes about Lodge "he steeled himself against the illusion of success, and bore with apparent and outward indifference the total indifference of the public," we may ask: Does one *bear it* if one does not care about it? Adams's language expresses the resentment of the scorned suitor.

Adams makes Bay Lodge the alienated artist, albeit an artist *manqué*, coming out of a social milieu which Ernest Samuels describes as the "*type bourgeois-bostonien* . . . introspective, deracinated, 'improvised Europeans.'" This *type* includes William Wetmore Story, maybe J. R. Lowell, Charles Eliot Norton, certainly Henry James, Henry Adams, and their pale successors like Logan Pearsall Smith—maybe half the bodies buried in Rome's Protestant Cemetery, among whom we find W. W. Story.

Now, Story was a bad sculptor, although better at sculpture than at poetry. Clover Adams wrote her father, after a honeymoon visit to Story's Roman studio, "oh! how he does spoil nice blocks of white marble. Nothing but Sibyls on all sides . . . all with the same expression as if they smelt something wrong."

Europe was full of the *type*, languid flowers of counter-emigration. However, at least two of its representatives mastered ironic prose to the point of literature—the one by nuance and architecture achieving *The Ambassadors*; the other his letters, his *History*, his *Education*, his *Chartres*, and in small his *Life of George Cabot Lodge*. I place his best sentences on a revolving stage, like sculpture in the round; in such prose—and not in poetry—Henry Adams could embody irony faceted with counterfeeling. The opening metaphor derives from the Lodge vacation retreat on the sea.

> . . . young Lodge's nature was itself as elementary and simple as the salt water. Throughout life, the more widely his character spread in circumference, the more simply he thought, and even when trying to grow complex—as was inevitable since it was to grow in Boston—the mind itself was never complex, and the complexities merely gathered on it, as something outside, like the sea-weeds gathering and swaying about the rocks. Robust in figure, healthy in appetite, careless of consequences, he could feel complex and introspective only as his ideal, the Norse faun, might feel astonished and angry at finding nature perverse and unintelligible in a tropical jungle. Since nature could not be immoral or futile, the immorality and futility must be in the mind that conceived it. Man became an outrage; society an artificial device for the distortion of truth; civilization a wrong. Many millions of simple natures have thought, and still think, the same thing, and the more complex have never quite made up their minds whether to agree with them or not; but the thought that was simple and sufficient for the Norseman exploring the tropics, or for an exuberant young savage sailing his boat off the rude shores of Gloucester and Cape Ann, could not long survive in the atmosphere of State Street. Commonly the poet dies young.

American poets at the end of the nineteenth century were incapable of such a cross-hatching of praise, condescension, sympathy, tenderness, and contempt—such a teeming vivacity of contradiction. For that matter, Whitman never approached the possibility, however he bragged of contradicting himself; only Dickinson fixed or registered such engines of internal opposition. If Adams could not be a poet, he could in such passages of prose approximate the poetic language of the seventeenth century in its stitching-and-unstitching of ambivalent intensity.

When Edmund Wilson calls Adams's *Lodge* "a dreary and cold little book"—yet places it in *The Shock of Recognition*—he enacts another American contradiction. This *Life* is not cold; if it is grudging, it is tender in its suppression of tenderness—as Adams's blankness about his wife, in his autobiography, indicates boiling not freezing. This *Life* makes bitter acknowledgment that Americans cannot write poetry. "Commonly the poet dies young," says Adams—and pretending a figure he states the letter: Trumbull Stickney died at thirty, Lodge at thirty-six, William Vaughan Moody at forty-three. Did State Street kill them all?

It did not kill the next batch. When Wilson wrote his introduction he pointed out that Adams remained ignorant of E. A. Robinson, born four years earlier than Bay Lodge in 1869. If Adams had read Robinson—a discovery of the savage Theodore Roosevelt—he would have remained unable to read him well. Wilson omits to notice that Robert Frost was Lodge's own age, born a year later, that Wallace Stevens was six years younger, that William Carlos Williams came four years after Stevens, and then the deluge: Pound, Moore, Doolittle, Eliot.

These poets were not the *type bourgeois-bostonien*. Some took Europe for model, some rejected it, some heard Whitman (without the limitation of fanaticism), some read Laforgue, some heard the Middle Ages or classic literatures. Although three went to Harvard, none came from Boston—for even Mr. Eliot had been raised by the Mississippi, two generations away from Beacon Hill, and only *cousin* to readers of the Boston *Transcript*.

ON MOVING ONE'S LIPS, WHILE READING

Miss Stephanie Ford stepped to the blackboard. My first-grade teacher was angular, elderly, and black-haired. (Once I heard a grown-up say, "She must *do* something to her hair," which bewildered me.) The day before, Miss Ford had announced, "Tomorrow, we will begin to learn to read." The whole school year, we had prepared for this day. It was a moment, I told myself at the age of six, that I would remember forever. My house was a temple of reading. Every night after supper, when my parents finished the afternoon newspaper, and my father the work he brought home from the office, they concealed their faces behind books. Reading was what grown-ups did; now I, eager to overcome the obstacle of childhood, would join the reading world.

Miss Ford drew a series of sharp lines, making large printed letters, which we had learned as the alphabet, stringing together T, H, A, and T—white on black. She stood back and raised her long wooden pointer. "That," she said in her stiff clear voice, "is 'that.'" If her enunciation was stiff, it was not cold, because she moved her lips in an exaggerated fashion—she opened her mouth wide; her tongue curled and snapped—so that we might understand or imitate the oral formation of sounds. This angular, elderly, black-haired person taught us to read by acts of mouth and body.

We had studied the alphabet for weeks, late in 1934, by chanting it aloud in unison and copying it in pencil on large yellowish lined sheets of paper. All through grammar school, much of our learning was memorization and repetition by rote, "two plus two is four," whatever the subject: state capitals, the presidents with their years of office. Eight years later, when we started Latin in high school, we singsonged "amo, amas, amat" for Mr. Brown who always wore brown. Meanwhile we repeated multiplication tables, the dates of battles, poems, the principal products of Portugal, and the Gettysburg Address.

We did not speak pieces competitively as our parents and grandparents had done; entertainment by movies and radio had replaced recitation of poems and oratory. A pity. Loss of recitation helped to detach words from the sounds they make, which is the castration of reading. This loss took the name of educational reform, which attacked not speaking pieces but the memorization required for speaking pieces. Beginning in the late 1920s, spreading over years into the educational trenches, American educators crusaded against memorization. Doubtless the crusade was in general good. There are better ways to learn history, social studies, and geography. Reasoning by rule is more useful for mathematics than memorizing tables for consultation. (As for balancing a checkbook, our calculators will do that for us.) Learning French or Spanish by talking it, or reading real examples of its literature, will bring us inside the syntax of a culture better than the rote imprint of conjugations.

But when they discarded recitation of dates and declensions, educators threw out as well the practice of reciting and performing literary work, and with it the habit of understanding literature by hearing it, by absorbing the noises it makes. In my earlier words about "Casey at the Bat," I praised the old culture that centered on the written word performed aloud for edification and entertainment. Before the automobile took farmers to the movies, before the radio's chatter ended the millennia of silences, our entertainment was local: piano solo, drama group, chorus, barbershop quartet—and recitation or performance of the written word.

When we looked at print a hundred years ago (or fifty, or whenever), we imbibed it as *sound* (with or without committing it to memory) at school or church, in nursery or living room. People performed literary art, or popular entertainment, even while doing other tasks. Memorization let the woodworker recite the "Raven" or "The Heathen Chinee" while turning a lathe, and the mother chant "Baa, baa black sheep" for her baby while her hands assembled a pie. On Sunday the preacher read from the book, prophet and gospel; on worknights after milking, an elocutionary cousin performed chapters from Scott and Dickens. At school we recited gems of political oratory and stanzas from the poets.

In a few blessed backwaters, school children still do prize speaking once a year. My town of Danbury, New Hampshire, is a surviving culture of the nineteenth century, like those Greek colonies in the Italian hills, founded four centuries before Christ, that still spoke Athenian Greek after World War II. Prize Speaking Night at Danbury School is a measure of what we were, a memory alive reconstituting the old world. I recommend it.

Technology exists to make memory unnecessary; we invented the alphabet so that we needed no longer memorize Homer. But the alphabet was a device for the preservation of noise not of information. For a long time the written poem was a mnemonic device for the poem itself—and the spoken poem was the poem. It was more than a thousand years before humans invented silent reading. Literature was something heard not seen. Almost until Gutenberg, literary performance (and perception) was sound not sight, mouth and ear not eye and mind. When silent reading became common, roughly during the Renaissance, literature flourished—but:

This silent reading remained a noisy matter.

Until recently, when we have read silently we have heard every word. Spending our childhoods listening to people read aloud or recite, ourselves reciting and performing in school and for the fun of it, we could not read in silence without inwardly hearing the words read. Even people too shy to read aloud heard print make noises in their heads.

Even now, if we read literature properly, we hear the words on the page—in our own minds. Hearing the words, we make constant unconscious decisions about tone, feeling, and import;

we remain alert to the gestures of words. Hearing the words, we cannot skim; passivity is impossible. By imagining how the words would sound if spoken aloud, we understand their tone. If we see on the page the sentence "Mr. Rumble nodded his head," our inward voicing requires us to understand whether Mr. Rumble disapproved, or was outraged, or merely passed on information ("No, it's not raining").

If we do not hear the words inside our heads, we are reading passively. Speed reading is sloppy reading, an abomination, and turns the reader into a slack-jawed receiver of surfaces, of mere information. We hear about Mr. Rumble's head gesture but we pass over its implication. When we allow words to be abstracted to the page or screen, detached from the body and the sensations of the human, we abandon the site of feelings. Do Mr. Rumble's palms sweat? Does he feel an erection starting? Does his toe hurt? Mr. Rumble looks bland and speaks without affect, like a voice generated by a computer. Who knows what Mr. Rumble is thinking?

Of course sometimes we need only information. By necessity all of us must learn a selective difference in modes of reading. We must read quickly in order to process newspapers, manuals of instruction, and business journals—or we would go crazy; it would take us a month to read the Sunday *Times* hearing every word. We would lose our minds if we listened with an inner ear to the instructions that come with 1040A.

On the other hand, when we read for joy—for beauty, for intelligence, for understanding—we must hear the words in order to read well. If we move our lips when we read silently, fine; it will slow us down, and we will read better. Whether moving our lips or not, we must test literature's words in our mouths. When I read good poems, in perfect silence, after twenty minutes my throat muscles feel tired.

Most people have become passive readers, and passive reading is diminished literacy. Television takes most of the blame, but there were earlier reasons: The motor car invented shopping and the movie, for Americans who lived outside cities; there was also radio, wonderful radio: We stopped singing for each other and let Rudy Vallee take over. We listened no more to public recitations of "Little Orphant Annie" because radio soap operas were available every day. We didn't need "The Owl and the Pussycat" because we had Fibber McGee and Molly.

But . . . when the automobile replaces walking, we need to take up jogging. We can learn to read again, and maybe to move our lips, by becoming conscious of the sound of words. The recent habit of taped books certainly helps. Commuting, we hear words acted, language made human by emphatic mouths, lips, and tongues. (It helps if the book is literature and entire.) Hearing books helps restore blood and flesh to language, bringing sound back to literary experience.

But, listening to tapes, we are only receptors: Actors are active for us; other voices, other minds make decisions of tone. Better is reading aloud ourselves, preferably as a regular part of the day, and such reading aloud is not only for parents entertaining children. My wife and I have read a hundred books aloud, thirty minutes a day of *Huckleberry Finn*, *Madame Bovary*, the *New Testament*, Fitzgerald's *Odyssey*, and enormous quantities of Henry James. It's our local perversity, perhaps, but we find late James superb on the tongue. I've read every syllable of *The Ambassadors* aloud twice. I've read aloud *Portrait of a Lady*, wonderful late stories like "The Beast in the Jungle," *The Golden Bowl*, and *Wings of the Dove*. Maybe they read aloud so well because James dictated them.

The voice that reads late James aloud may not be monotone. To read parenthesis within parenthesis, the reader must drop pitches and build them up again, and a sentence by Henry James becomes an exercise for voice-athletes to train by, pitches and pauses in particular. Representing James by your mouth, lips, tongue, contracted throat, and vocal cords, you accomplish literary analysis by means of your vocal equipment. Your larynx could write a doctoral thesis on the Jamesian parenthesis.

This reading aloud, and this association of words with sounds, started for me when I was small: my mother reading aloud from *Silver Pennies*; my grandfather reciting "Casey" and a thousand other funny, sentimental, and melodramatic poems. I was lucky to be born while traces of the old culture survived. It survived also in Miss Stephanie Ford with her exaggerated mouthing of T-H-A-T. We learned to read by moving our lips— and tongue and larynx—and "that was that" for literacy and ultimately literature. If reading, and the love of literature, continues, we need again to connect words with the noises they make in our mouths.

THE DARKENED PARLOR

The *Oxford English Dictionary* confirms—what we'd guess from Parliament and *parler*—that parlors started as places for talking, rooms in monasteries where monks could speak to visitors. Soon aristocrats used the word for a private conversation place, separate from the public great hall. Not until the nineteenth century, it appears, did the word come to mean our parlor: "the 'best room' distinct from the ordinary living room." By 1880, the *Scientific American* could boast that in the United States "almost every well-to-do mechanic has his parlor, or 'best room.'"

None of these sources mention one common use of parlors, at least in New England. In Robert Frost's "Home Burial," the grieving mother reproaches her husband's insensitivity by referring to "what was in the darkened parlor." Their dead boy's body lay there, and bodies lay in parlors for New England centuries as long as funerals took place in people's houses. When we changed our burying habits, we called the undertaker's establishment a funeral parlor.

My family never used parlors for much else. Sometimes we've used them for weddings, sometimes for sickness, sometimes for courting (a heatless parlor encouraged hugging), and sometimes for coffee when the minister came. The parlor at our place is a pretty room, but in my grandparents' day, the furniture was uncomfortable—parlor furniture was by definition uncomfortable—acknowledging that the room was not for daily life. Now we keep a loveseat there—it turns into a bed for solitary visitors—and a recliner for a mother's arthritic back. Even though we fill it with comfort, even though it's our prettiest room, we seldom sit there.

It's the southwest corner of the original Cape, with windows that gather southern and western light. Because the Grafton Turnpike widened to become Route 4, the western windows front on a busy road, which makes it noisy with pickups at dawn and dusk all year, and noisier all summer with the traffic of vacationers. We use it as a gallery for family pictures, grandparents and even great-grandparents, mostly photographs but one silhouette of a great-great-great, and one pastel of my grandmother looking beautiful and idealized at twenty. Around the wall there's the original wooden chair-rail, to keep us from denting plaster. Against the inside wall there's a fake fireplace, with a parallel fake in my study—the opposite room at the house's northwest corner. Our false fireplaces puzzle me. The house is old enough for real fireplaces but there's no structural evidence, down in the rootcellar, that we ever had them. The rootcellar is clearly as old as the house, with 1803 bark clinging to beams with an adze's mark.

Why did we ever need a parlor, with the comfortable living room adjacent? All over New England, old houses carry this extra room; and no new house gets built with one. Sometimes in a made-over old house we find an unusual enormous living room—evidence that a modern owner, after the advent of central heat, conflated living room with parlor. It makes a room like the aristocrat's great hall, large enough for presidential candidates during quadrennial coffee hours.

My grandmother Kate put our parlor to practical use, for twenty years, when she ran a part-time business. Many farm wives, in families perpetually long on land and short on cash, raised money with a sideline. My grandmother made and sold hats, calling her work by a fancy name: In a photograph on one of my bookjackets there's a one-word legend over this house's front door: *millinery*. Nobody can read it because the publisher printed the photograph backward.

Poking around in our back chamber, I once came across a thicket of iron pins that stuck upright ten inches from a round base, objects that bewildered me until I realized: These hat stands stood on tables Kate erected in the parlor, fall and spring, when she opened her shop. Neighbor women pulled up their buggies and stopped inside to try the new fashions in hats. Sometimes Kate hitched up her own buggy and drove her millinery to remote farms in the hills. She not only sold new hats, store-bought and homemade, but refurbished old ones—a new veil, an artificial flower—for true Yankees who wouldn't buy something new when they could make over something old.

Twice a year Kate took the train to Boston, to check out the new fashions, to buy hats and hat-material. When my mother was a little girl, sometimes she accompanied her mother to the city on these millinery expeditions. At ninety my mother Lucy still remembers an enormous Woolworth's with its long, long, long counter of penny toys; she could pick any one she wanted.

The Model T ended the parlor's commerce. People drove to Franklin (fourteen miles away, population five thousand) to shop for millinery, and everything in the universe, at its department store, Holmes and Nelson, where the change scooted from cashier to clerk by a tiny trolley that hurtled along wire tracks. This vast emporium, oddly enough, has shrunk into a Western Auto.

When my parents were married in the living room in 1927, their wedding presents sat on tables in the parlor. In some houses, people were married in the parlor—the same places they were buried out of—but ordinary life never inhabited parlors. When the family gathered in the ordinary evening, they gathered around a central table in the living room, warm in winter from the Glenwood, where a high bright oil lamp cast its light. Some read books; some did homework; sometimes one elocutionist read aloud while others sewed and listened. The girls practiced fancy work they learned from their Aunt Nannie. My grandmother mostly darned, repaired, tatted, knitted, crocheted—and for twenty years made hats. Everybody kept *busy*, in the living room—and the parlor stayed empty, the door closed in winter, shades drawn in summer, useless . . .

Or nearly. When Aunt Nannie went crazy, she was crazy in the parlor. I remember the scary summer of 1938 when I was nine: senile dementia, screams and long disconnected monologues. She died in September, buried the day before the hurricane, and her coffin set in the parlor. When my grandfather Wesley died fifteen years later, his coffin was the last to set there. My grandmother, who lived until 1975 and ninety-seven, was buried out of our church two miles down the road by the same undertaker—who was so pleased at how well he prepared my grandfather that he took Kodachrome slides of Wesley in his coffin.

My mother remembers that it was Aunt Nannie who stayed up all night with Nannie's father's body, my great-grandfather Ben Keneston, when he died in 1913. Somebody stayed up all night in the parlor with the corpse, my mother tells me; it was only one night, because they put them in the ground quickly those days, before the country culture embraced embalming. You stayed up all night, she adds, just in case . . . You don't want a cat wandering in there. I say: But I thought cats weren't allowed in the house, back then; they patrolled the barn and the grainshed. Well, my mother said, maybe someone stayed up, just in case, you know, a rat . . .

Sometimes, late in the day, when the western sun sheds its canary-light across the floor, Jane and I sit reading in the parlor, enjoying Kearsarge handsome through the south window. But mostly we let the parlor remain a people-free zone, a room set to the side of the ordinary life. Maybe it's good to preserve a best room—for rituals of courtship and marriage, for disease and dying—to remind ourselves how central they are, these matters on the periphery of our lives.

GRAVEYARD PEOPLE

Walking or driving Route 4 in New Hampshire, we come upon little graveyards every few miles. When we leave the paved two-lane highway, for the dirt roads that curve uphill taking us back country, sometimes we find minuscule stone-walled burial grounds that served one family. In the tiny towns hereabouts, voters each year elect a citizen trustee of grave-yards, seeing to it that available funds (small endowments or line items in the town budget) keep them properly trim and tidy.

In Andover there's an eighteenth-century acre where my old-est New Hampshire ancestors lie, and past it the large Proctor Cemetery to take care of the nineteenth and twentieth centuries. In one or the other lie my grandparents, some of my great-grandparents, back to some great-great-greats. Here Jane and I, a dozen years back, bought ourselves a place near a ravine, un-der great birches and white pines. Sometimes I walk the dog in Proctor—any excuse to haunt a graveyard—though never on a Sunday, not to mention on Memorial Day: Gus's devotional micturition could prove offensive.

Sometimes Jane and I walk on a dirt road past Andover center, off Route 11 on the way to Franklin. A couple of miles in, without a house around, we mosey in a small graveyard with or without the dog, reading inscriptions and imagining past lives. Jane discovered here the early nineteenth-century grave of Samuel Smith, his stone standing among the stones of his three wives—all named Susan. This is a place of many Smiths, of Swett and Fifield, of Downes and Morrill, of Clay, Clark, Sleeper, and Cilley. Many local citizens bear these names; many of these names flutter among the leaves of my family tree.

Down the road from our house, only half a mile, there's a little burying ground set on a slope; each marker digs five or six inches deeper into the ground on its northern end. Afternoon sun colors the granite tawny and points sharp shadows on the hill. (When I pass this graveyard, late afternoon in leaf season, someone has always parked to use a camera.) But why is this graveyard here, far from a church, with houses only every half-mile? A Wilmot historian lets us guess, telling us that this area was East Wilmot once. We live in a small flap of Wilmot that tucks across Route 4 between Danbury and Andover. We were to be East Wilmot, making with Wilmot Flat, North Wilmot, and Wilmot Center a quadripartite township. It turns out that some citizens, after the Civil War and before the Spanish, planned a church here; and I suppose that this cemetery is a churchyard that never acquired its church. Here I find Brown, Currier, Sleeper again, Waldron, Tilton, Braley, Charles Scales 1842–1902 of the 18th N.H. infantry, and Bussell as well as Buswell, which is the same as Buzzle—and Boswell for that matter.

A mile further north, just this side of our South Danbury

Christian Church, my grandpaternal great-grandparents lie in the half-acre South Danbury Churchyard. My grandfather's father John Wells lies here, 1841–1927, veteran of the Civil War, who flies a small frayed flag like so many of the New Hampshire dead: "Co. F., 15th Reg. N.H. Vols." An iron rail surrounds this place protecting Currier, Sleeper, Cilley, and Morrill again, as well as other names I count among neighbors and cousins: Peaslee, Huntoon, Stevens, Pinard, Ford, Glidden—I visit Ella Glidden's grave, beautiful old woman I knew as a child at church, widow of a farmer who hanged himself in his barn—Langley, Eastman, and Perkins. For decades this graveyard hunkered under low hills dense with black-green hemlock, protected by arboreal darkness and comforted by the density of black-green embrace. A developer cut them down and the graveyard seems vulnerable now.

Graveyards are most taking when we least expect them. As we drive up Kearsarge, toward the half-way spot where we can picnic or park to climb, I am startled every time to catch sight of a beautiful small densely shaded graveyard. It takes my breath away to park here and walk among the eighteenth- and nineteenth-century slabs of granite and slate. How could they have farmed up here, with the land so high and cold and scrappy? Farm they did, as the stone walls tell us, and cellar-holes when we walk in the woods. Old people still remember the one-room Kearsarge schoolhouse that stood on this road. How beautiful it must have been up here, and how isolated in winter, for the long generations of these bones.

For the most part, we no longer live close enough to graveyards. Doubtless this failing accounts for crime, drugs, racism,

the S & L scandal, and Senator Helms. When we live by a graveyard, we enjoy quiet neighbors, yes, but neighbors eloquent to
remind us of our present end. Sensible people agree: A day
spent without the thought of death is a wasted day. The sight of
a gravestone, weighty not only in its granite, allows us perspec-
tive on problems as pressing as burnt toast, taxes, and
headcolds.

Village people kept their churchyards nearby, like the dead
field at Stoke Poges that Thomas Gray celebrated:

> Beneath those rugged elms, that yew-tree's shade,
> Where heaves the turf in many a mould'ring heap,
> Each in his narrow cell for ever laid,
> The rude Forefathers of the hamlet sleep.

The eighteenth century in England produced a whole school of
graveyard poets, Gray the latest and best. In America the elegy—especially over the death of a child—became the most
common poem of the nineteenth century. (When Lydia Sigour-
ney collected a book of seventy such laments, Mark Twain
claimed that she had added a new terror to death.) Reading the
names and dates of the old stones, as we root around in bone-
yards, we note the omnipresence of death for our ancestors—so
many dead children, so many wives dead and husbands remarried and new dead infants of new brides. Is it by a reaction, now,
that we avoid any confrontation with death? Contemporary memorial institutions—like Forest Lawn—attest to avoidance
only.

It's not only New Hampshire that makes beautiful or touching
graveyards. For a couple of years I lived in the English village

of Thaxted, not Stoke Poges but prettier, where wild graves thrived in their tussocky beauty around the great fifteenth-century church. I wandered among them every day, passing the almshouses to get there, leaving by a gate down Stony Lane, which *was* a stony lane, past medieval townhouses where stone-workers lived for two centuries building the church.

In Rome my favorite place is the Protestant Cemetery. We went there first, like everybody, to see Keats's grave, beside Shelley's, near the first-century pyramid of Cestius where Rome's stray cats congregate. On our first visit, after homage to the poets we discovered the densely populated main part of the cemetery, and I wandered among the dead I had read about in twenty years of leafing among late-nineteenth-century letters and biography—those great generations of Europeanized Americans and Romantic Englishmen, sculptors and forgotten novelists and painters, remembered by readers of Henry James's letters or Henry Adams's. These English and American artists, Roman dilettantes, ended residing in the damp, shady, crowded, cat-ridden, monumental alleys of the Protestant Cemetery. I walk among them as if I were reading leisurely Victorian letters or weekending at the villas and country houses of the fastidious dead.

But we care most for home granite. Especially I love that Andover acre where my oldest ancestors remain. My great-grandfather, who resides in Proctor Cemetery, was Benjamin Cilley Keneston. His father was plain Benjamin, distinguished from his son by the giddy vacancy of Cilley, who lies in the tiny old graveyard as he otherwise inhabits our parlor, in the shape of a daguerreotype and a photograph.

The former shows him looking young, but he was born in 1789 and Daguerre didn't invent his process until 1839, so he wasn't young; his hair is as long as a hippie's around a meaty sensuous face, and his young-looking bride beside him grins with an expression like a leer. The photograph shows the same man old, same vigorous hair but the eyes wild and cheekbones stark. It must have been a difficult life. I know that the handsome young woman in the earlier photograph died, and Benjamin married her sister; I know that children died: This morning I walked again in the graveyard to check it out; yes, he buried two daughters, each dead at nineteen—Abigail from his first wife Miriam dead in 1836; Elvira from his second wife Hannah dead in 1842. Benjamin himself lasted until the middle of the war, joining his daughters in 1863. Near him in the old graveyard is his father Jonathan, who fought in the Revolution, my great-great-great. Before Jonathan? Stone records dim out. My personal interest dims out also, when I cannot couple the dead with a house, or a plot of land, or visit their graves.

But there's no need to know the dead personally, or to be descended from them, to enjoy their company in their last places. It's peaceful to loiter among representatives of the majority, in Roman cities or in English villages or down the road, acknowledging with serenity that we will join their ranks. In "Church Going" Philip Larkin, writing as an agnostic, spoke of churches and their surrounding yards as "places to grow wise in / If only that so many dead lie round."

BLUEJEANS
AND ROBERT FRANCIS

The woods of New England were crowded with hermits, when I was a boy; if you traveled dirt roads in the hills, you had to watch out or you might trip over one. Everywhere men devoted to the solitary life built camps, shot coons, grew peas, raised heifers, and worked on the roads to pay their taxes. No longer do we find these unmonkish hermits on every byway. Perhaps they became stockbrokers.

In western Massachusetts one of the great solitaries died not long ago, at a good age: an old poet who loved sunbathing, low overhead, and soybeans. Robert Francis designed his own two-and-a-half-room house, "Fort Juniper," just outside Amherst, Massachusetts—where another solitary poet once haunted her own house wearing a white dress and making quatrains. Francis lived through much of the twentieth century, 1901 to 1987, although he never entirely belonged to it. He was ahead of his time, pacifist and vegetarian, a soybean laureate who served us soybean cookies and Fort Juniper tea (comfrey, lemon balm, spearmint) when my wife and I called on him some years before he died. Most of his food like his daily life was homemade, but he had nothing against technology except for its waste and its expense. He wrote directly onto a typewriter, nine books of poetry and numerous prose books that touched the edges of poetry. He went without modern conveniences because he kept his overhead low—and low overhead was a moral matter. Late in his life, for reasons of health, he installed a telephone. When Henry Lyman first saw the instrument at his friend's house, he was surprised. "Oh," he said, "you have a telephone."

Old Robert glanced at the object as if it were an intruder. "It's doing pretty well," he said. Nonetheless, callers sometimes discovered a large cushion muffling the instrument.

Here are two late poems published after his death:

Nursery Song

The moon, the moon is Peeping Tom
At every window in the town,
And half the shades are up for him
And half the shades are down.

Dark windows in the lee of light
He reaches all of them in time,
For Tom is out for all the night
And Tom knows how to climb.

Cadence

Puckered like an old apple she lies abed,
Saying nothing and hearing nothing said,
Not seeing the birthday flowers by her head
To comfort her. She is not comforted.

The room is warm, too warm, but there is chill
Over her eyes and over her tired will.

Her hair is frost in the valley, snow on the hill.
Night is falling and the wind is still.

Francis had many friends but he loved solitude as much as he loved his friends. A sign on the door, taped beside a stiff-bristled brush hanging from a peg, asked visitors please to clean the soles of their shoes before they entered. The hermits of my childhood were not so fastidious.

Inside Fort Juniper he kept a small refrigerator and a Charm Crawford stove, converted in 1941 from wood-or-coal to kerosene. When the Charm Crawford died of old age, Robert submitted to propane. (Everyone lamented the Charm Crawford's demise except for Robert Francis.) Otherwise this small house, on a wooded knoll off Market Hill Road, contained a small desk, a secretary, two filing cabinets, two tables, bookshelves, a sofa, and four chairs—one of which Francis had extracted from a Model A.

In 1977 he had a stroke. When he didn't answer a daily telephone call, one September day in 1979, a neighbor looked through the open door of Fort Juniper to find Robert sprawled on the floor. "Are you all right, Bob?" said his neighbor. "No!!!" roared Francis, who had suffered another stroke but would not suffer a foolish question; he asked if his neighbor thought he always slept on the floor. His neighbor said that he didn't know *how* poets slept; Francis answered that he was "a very *orderly* poet." *Then* the ambulance came.

The Oxen

Massive, submissive, mute
The yoked oxen stand
Waiting the rod's touch

So in the Iliad
While the rod rested, so
In the Old Testament

With those benign great eyes
Gazing as they now gaze
At something beyond time.

He tapped his own maple trees. He brewed dandelion wine. In the last years of his life, he ate the same menu every day: for breakfast juice, oatmeal, whole wheat toast, and one egg; for lunch macaroni and cheese plus soybeans; for dinner soybeans plus macaroni and cheese. He did not own a garbage pail, because he endured no leftover food. Eggshells and orange peels he kept until he walked in the woods where he scattered them. He saved plastic bags and jars for his own use, or gave them to someone who could use them. Tin cans were rare events; occasionally he bagged two or three, and passed them to a friend for recycling.

A visitor mentioned to Robert Francis that coffee would be served after a new series of poetry readings. Francis remarked that, over the years, he had drunk many cups of coffee at the library at Amherst College. He left the room and reappeared with a shoebox full of washed plastic spoons.

Here is a poem from his youth:

Good Night Near Christmas

And now good night. Good night to this old house
Whose breathing fires are banked for their night's rest.
Good night to lighted windows in the west.
Good night to neighbors and to neighbors' cows

Whose morning milk will be beside my door.
Good night to one star shining in. Good night

> To earth, poor earth with its uncertain light,
> Our little wandering planet still at war.
>
> Good night to one unstarved and gnawing mouse
> Between the inner and the outer wall.
> He has a paper nest in which to crawl.
> Good night to men who have no bed, no house.

All his life he loved to lie naked in the sun. When he built Fort Juniper he made the roof a sundeck; he climbed there on a ladder. When he was old he sat naked in a chair behind a clump of trees. The year he died he still sunbathed, wearing only shoes and, on occasion, a hat.

After his strokes his eyesight deteriorated until he was legally blind. He dictated poems and prose to friends. At poetry readings he spoke his work from memory.

> Nothing Is Far
>
> Though I have never caught the word
> Of God from any calling bird,
> I hear all that the ancients heard.
>
> Though I have seen no deity
> Enter or leave a twilit tree,
> I see all that the seers see.
>
> A common stone can still reveal
> Something not stone, not seen, yet real.
> What may a common stone conceal?
>
> Nothing is far that once was near.
> Nothing is hid that once was clear.
> Nothing was God that is not here.
>
> Here is the bird, the tree, the stone.
> Here in the sun I sit alone
> Between the known and the unknown.

When he was middle-aged he kept a pet hen called Gladys in Fort Juniper's fireplace. For verification and detail, the reader should consult an autobiography, *The Trouble with Francis*, where Gladys is listed in an "Index of Persons Named."

Mostly the reader—*any* reader—should dwell upon his *Collected Poems* of 1976, Robert Francis's beautiful exact renderings of the creation he observed, touched, and celebrated. This creation includes baseball, which Francis wrote about as well as anyone—crafty lyrics about pitchers and base stealers—although he never cared for the game.

> The Base Stealer
>
> Poised between going on and back, pulled
> Both ways taut like a tightrope-walker,
> Fingertips pointing the opposites,
> Now bouncing tiptoe like a dropped ball
> Or a kid skipping rope, come on, come on,
> Running a scattering of steps sidewise,
> How he teeters, skitters, tingles, teases,
> Taunts them, hovers like an ecstatic bird,
> He's only flirting, crowd him, crowd him,
> Delicate, delicate, delicate, delicate—now!

Henry Lyman tells a story about Robert and bluejeans. In 1983 Robert decided that it might be time to buy another pair, which came as a relief to his friends who had been watching the current trousers deteriorate for a decade. Robert arranged for the Senior Surrey to take him to the mall in Hadley, and there he found a store willing to sell him a new pair. But when he tried to put them on, they were so stiff that he could not drag them over his legs. Doubtless with relief, he decided instead to buy a patch for his old bluejeans. The store charged him fifty cents for the patch—and then the clerk attempted to add a sales tax. *No*, Robert politely and firmly insisted; he would *not* pay the sales tax: After all, a patch was an article of clothing and thus not subject to Massachusetts tax. The manager was summoned, the argument repeated, and in the end Robert prevailed. He saved three cents and one moral principle.

One more poem, from middle age:

> Hide-and-Seek
>
> Here where the dead lie hidden
> Too well ever to speak,
> Three children unforbidden
> Are playing hide-and-seek.
>
> What if for such a hiding
> These stones were not designed?
> The dead are far from chiding;
> The living need not mind.
>
> Too soon the stones that hid them
> Anonymously in play
> Will learn their names and bid them
> Come back to hide to stay.

When Francis's old bluejeans split, despite the half-dollar patch, Henry Lyman provided him an old pair of his own. Robert praised their softness.

ART FOR LIFE FOR ART

When the election results looked certain, November of 1992, my friend Bailey, who works in finance but withholds himself from the Republican Party, telephoned for mutual congratulations. With excitement I mentioned that President Clinton would make good appointments in the arts—to run the National Endowment, for instance. Bailey laughed at my provincialism; *his* major worries are deficits and entitlements. "Art's not exactly my top priority," he said . . . Yet when Bailey went home, he returned to a vast CD collection, a houseful of objects of art, and a thousand books. He went home to read good prose in a well-designed chair under a handsome print while he listened to music. Or maybe Bailey and his wife went out that night, to catch Eric Bogosian in performance, or to hear a jazz quintet. He lives breathing art's air without understanding the priority art occupies in his life.

For me it's obvious enough: In the early morning, I try to produce art; the rest of my day, I tend to consume it. I take art in—like many people—in order to keep myself sane and whole and reasonably happy. Art is a pleasure, but unlike simpler plea-sures—say, an ice-cream cone; say, the National Basketball As-sociation—art enhances human consciousness; it organizes the sensibility, discovering order and shape in the multiplicity of ex-perience; without good art and design around us, our minds fray among a welter of unrelated particulars. I claim for art in general what William Carlos Williams claimed for poems: that "men die miserably every day / for lack / of what is found there." Art is for life is for art is for life.

It's common to condescend to art—as not possessing the highest priority—even among people whose daily lives are most lightened and lit by it. Doubtless as Eratosthenes in fifth-century Athens walked home with Laodice from a government-sponsored Sophoclean performance, past sculpture and archi-tecture commissioned from Pheidias and Ictinus by Periclean gold, he deplored spending the treasury's wealth on painting while some citizens in this great democracy were so poor that they could hardly keep a slave.

Doubtless, Laodice agreed that we should not fund a dance company because of the homeless; that we should withhold money from orchestras because crack cocaine rules city streets; that we should starve art museums in order to nurture medical research. In the perennial song of the urgencies, art is always expendable. There's never a moment when we cannot name something more essential to support than a picture or a song or a story; yet we live and die, we understand ourselves and others, we cherish and extend our humanity by stories, pictures, and songs. Art is a source of the compassion by which we prefer funding misery over funding the arts.

We take art for granted, as if it were *there* like a hill or a wild-flower, as if it flourished naturally and without human care. We retreat when art is attacked; when bigots trash the National Endowment for the Arts, even political liberals suggest that the government retreat from supporting art: The art-kitchen gets hot, so we suggest burning down the kitchen. If Pericles had listened to David Brinkley or Eratosthenes, there would be no Parthenon—and without a Parthenon, without a Delphic charioteer, without an *Oedipus Rex*, we would be worse off than we are. Because of occasional victories by know-nothings and iconoclasts, we *are* worse off than we might have been: Barbarians (senators, columnists) melt the statues down; continually, we model the statues again—to magnify human consciousness.

Art has always needed public support. Renaissance painting and sculpture rose from the treasuries of princes both secular and sacred; opera, symphony, and dance came from the fortunes of the dukes and squires of Europe. Art has never supported itself; art is no virtuous merchant surviving in the marketplace by selling tickets or charging admission. In Europe, ticket sales account for twenty percent of the costs of music, dance, and the performing arts. In America, these sales account for as much as forty percent: no more than that, and the rest comes from patronage.

Without democracy, rich rulers hold power by wealth and wealth by power; with democracy, taxation collects popular power. Our enormous country used to support artistic institutions only in cities where rich patrons concentrated. In the last twenty-five years, through government seed money administered by the National Endowment, opera companies (and small publishers and art museums and regional theatres) have flourished in smaller cities from coast to coast. These institutions in their turn serve rural places: I have watched dancers from the Boston Ballet perform in the old opera house of Newport, New Hampshire. There it was—the beauty of the body in motion, available to anyone—at Newport's Opera House. So it is in the open places of Oklahoma and Idaho; so it is in industrial Ohio and Michigan.

We need the arts everywhere—among soybeans and highrises, among inner cities and rollingmills—to enhance our lives, even to reconcile us to our condition. Be it jazz or tragedy, art expands consciousness, and this enlargement is a goal to live for. Art makes apprehensible shapes out of random natural sources. Take all the sounds possible to the world, from birdsong to foghorn, organize the sound by scale and tempo, and sound turns into music. Replying, music organizes our ears to hear birdsong and foghorn. Literature derives from a haphazard of smells, visions, motives, and emotions—ordered by imagination and skilled language into purpose and resolution. Design, as well as great painting, informs the vision, making shapes by arranging the available manyness of color and form. Art extends human consciousness by capturing and making comprehensible the welter of sensations, sounds, and stories.

In the millennia since civilization divided labor, our jobs have specialized and isolated us from a view of the whole world. If we are lucky, our work can provide satisfaction—to teach kindergarten; to provide life insurance; to build bowling alleys and pickup trucks—but no job reaches into all crannies of the soul;

at least there remains room for other matter to enlarge and extend us, a necessity that art fills. What do we do, after we come home from office, school, factory, or bowling alley? We eat, we drink, we play with our children. Better we eat good food from plates that are shapely—better for the quality of consciousness: Design is nutrition for mind as food for body. Children's toys are beautiful or they are ugly; choosing the toys our children live with, we choose the mental ambience they grow up in. Apprehension of beauty in ordinary things—teacups, teddybears, and pillowcases—shapes the sensibility.

Art affects us when we don't notice it and when we do. In my own art of language, poetry is the extreme of arrangement: But the mathematics of poetry's formal resolution does not preclude moral thought, or satisfaction in honest naming, or the consolation of shared feeling. When someone dear to me dies, I go back to the seventeenth-century poets for consolation. Their stanzas are extremes of beauty and control, but language thrives elsewhere as well: We may discover a prose arithmetic of satisfaction in great novels or in the daily press. Sometimes I read reviews of rock music in the *Globe*—or Greil Marcus in the *Voice*—despite my musical ignorance, in order to take pleasure in the justice of syntax or epithet.

We consume art when we witness opera or listen to folk guitar; we consume it in the afternoon we spend at the art museum. Many also produce: learning to throw a pot; or working with a committee on the design of the library addition; or in the office attending to the language of a brochure. We produce arts or crafts when we sew or build, with or without a modicum of talent, and we learn better to read (or hear or see) a medium in which we participate; the best cook is the best taster.

No one can produce all the time, and Picasso sat still to hear the guitar. We consume art to strengthen the mind's precincts and the soul's avenues, making a city for living in—for the whole of our lives and for our lives' wholeness. No one is born sensitive to all art; we may improve and enlarge our pleasures by extending borders of appreciation. If we appreciate jazz but feel deaf to symphonic music, an exercise of attention will accrue accessible joy. Dutch painting, contemporary poetry, African woodcarving—the eras and genres of the world open themselves to pleasure through understanding. Life is for art is for life.

But if art be not continuous into the present day, our dilettantish appreciation of the past will separate us from our own day's air and policy. To the practiced sensibility, past art remains present while present art brings the past closer. Privately, we owe it to ourselves to be open to a continuum of the arts; publicly, it is our responsibility to enable the arts of our own day. It is only self-serving to support the arts, to support political candidates who disdain demagogic art-bashing, to support both federal and private underwriting of music, painting, theatre, literature, dance, sculpture, and design. Is this elitist? Only in the service of dragging everybody, kicking and screaming, into an elite of pleasure and understanding.

THE UNSAYABLE SAID

Poems are pleasure first: bodily pleasure, a deliciousness of the senses. Mostly, poems end by saying something (even the unsayable) but they start as the body's joy, like making love. Sometimes a poem remains a small pleasing sensation:

> Baa, baa, black sheep,
> Have you any wool?
> Yes, sir. Yes, sir.
> Three bags full.

Maybe these words once referred to taxation, but we hear them now without being tempted to paraphrase. Instead, we *chew* on them, *taste* them, and *dance* to them. This banquet or ballet starts in the crib, before arithmetic or thought. Everyone was once an infant who took mouth-pleasure in gurgle and shriek, accompanied by muscle-joy as our small limbs clenched and unclenched. Poetry starts from the crib; a thousand years later, John Donne makes lovers into compasses, T. S. Eliot contemplates the still point of the turning world, and Elizabeth Bishop remembers sitting as a child in the dentist's waiting room; but if these poets did not retain the mouth-pleasure of a baby's autistic utterance—pleasure in vowels on the tongue, pleasure in changes of volume and pause: *Baa, baa, black sheep*—we would not hear their meditations and urgencies.

The body is poetry's door; the sounds of words—throbbing in legs and arms; rich in the mouth—let us into the house.

Styles of architecture: In his spiritual grammar, Walt Whitman often wrote long complex sentences: The first sentence of "Out of the Cradle" is two hundred and eight words, arranged into twenty-two lines so that its subject, verb, and object wait until the last three lines. But the same poet could make a poem both brief and simple: This is "A Farm Picture"—all of it:

> Through the ample open door of the peaceful country barn,
> A sunlit pasture field with cattle and horses fading,
> And haze and vista, and the far horizon fading away.

It's merely a picture, an incomplete sentence—yet if we read it with an appropriate slow sensuous attentiveness, these lines fill us with a luminous beauty. The reader's mouth dwells in luxury on the three long *ay*s of the last line, but pleasure does not reside only in the mouth: Feel the balance in the first two lines—three and three, three and three—then the slight variation in the last line, with "haze and vista" and "far horizon fading away." The mouth lolls among dipthongs like a sunbather.

Readers who enjoy this small poem don't think about its balances and variations; we *feel* them, the way we feel a musical theme that returns slightly altered: expectation fulfilled and denied. With this poem as with the black sheep, we don't paraphrase; we take "A Farm Picture" for what it calls itself. But if we notice that the poem first appeared as the Civil War was ending in 1865, we may find the word "peaceful" emphatic. We speculate; speculation does no harm when it acknowledges itself. What the reader must not do (and what the classroom often encourages): We must never assume that the poem, appearing simple, hides an intellectual statement that only professors are equipped to explicate.

Yet, it's true: When we read poems we often feel more emotion than we can reasonably account for. If Whitman's little poem pleases us much, it pleases us more than paraphrase can explain. (To paraphrase this poem we are driven to synonyms— "Through the wide unclosed portal"—which serve only to show that synonyms do not exist.) Feeling bodily pleasure and fulfillment, feeling rightness beyond reason, feeling contentment or even bliss—we cannot account for the extremity of our satisfaction. By its art of saying the unsayable, poetry produces a response in excess of the discernible stimulus.

Pursuing the architectural analogy, I want to call this response the secret room. Friends of ours bought an old house in the country, a warren of small rooms, and after they furnished it and settled down, they became aware that their floor plan made no sense. Peeling off some wallpaper they found a door that pried open to reveal a tiny room, sealed off and hidden, goodness knows why: They found no corpses nor stolen goods. The unsayable builds a secret room, in the best poems, which shows in the excess of feeling over paraphrase. This room is not a Hidden Meaning, to be paraphrased by the intellect; it conceals itself from reasonable explanation. The secret room is something to acknowledge, accept, and honor in a silence of assent; the secret room is where the unsayable gathers, and it is poetry's uniqueness.

Poets are literal-minded, and poetry depends, even when it names marvelous and impossible things, on a literal mind. On the other hand, the conventional intellect wants to translate particulars into abstractions, as if images were allegorical; such translation is the grave error of the philosophers. The unsayable speaks only through the untranslated image and its noises. When we read Blake's "O Rose, thou art sick!" it is useless to ask, "What does *Rose* mean? What does *sick* mean?" Good readers imagine a rose and entertain notions of illness, possibly beginning with a plant canker and continuing to a blossom on a breathing tube, or—more historically—petals bled by leeches. When Emily Dickinson writes that "Death . . . kindly stopped for me," we listen to a story in which a horse and carriage—the figure of mortality holding the reins—pause to pick up a walker. Thomas Hardy, wandering as an old man in a graveyard, speculates on the vegetation growing from graves: Parts of a yew tree must be somebody his grandfather knew, because the yew grows from the burial place. Wandering further he sees a bush by the grave of a girl he knew when he was a young man:

> And the fair girl long ago
> Whom I often tried to know
> May be entering this rose.

Here we have two kinds of literalness: Hardy speculates on molecular survival, particles of the girl's body turned into botanical nutrients; but take the lines into the imagination, and we watch her molecules *enter* the rose as a living woman might walk through the portals of a church. The poetry, saying the unsayable, resides in the two ways of seeing or understanding brought (impossibly) together.

Anything that can be thoroughly said in prose might as well be said in prose. The everyday intellect remains satisfied with abstraction and prose; the poetic mentality wants more. In narrative poems, the poetry adds the secret (unsayable) room of feeling and tone to the sayable story. Philosophy in its more logical incarnations strives to eliminate powers of association because they are subjective and uncontrollable. Poetry, on the other hand, wants to address *the whole matter of the human*—including fact and logic, but also the body with its senses, and above all the harsh complexities of emotion. Our senses, excited by sound and picture, assimilate records of feeling that are also passages to feeling. Poems tell stories; poems recount ideas; but poems *embody* feeling. Because emotion is illogical—in logic opposites cannot both be true; in the life of feeling, we love and hate together—the poem exists to say the unsayable. Contradictory reality, represented in language, depends on nice distinctions. If Hardy told us that the fair girl "Might be marching into this cactus," his associations would have failed him—and we would not read his poem. Marianne Moore finds poetry in definition: "Nor was he insincere in saying, 'Make my house your inn.' / Inns are not residences." Sometimes definitions, plain in talk, combine logical impossibility with ironic witness, as in Geoffrey Hill:

> this is a raging solitude of desire,
> this is the chorus of obscene consent,
> this is the single voice of perfect praise.

Poems embody the coexistence of opposites that together form an identity; the Roman poet Catullus wrote *odi et amo*: "I hate and I love."

We come to poetry for the pleasure of its body and for the accuracy and confirmation of its feeling. When I grieve I go to poems that grieve; but mostly we read poetry for the love of it, not in search of consolation. In the act of reading, we exercise or practice emotion, griefs and joys, erotic transport and the anguish of loss—as if poems were academies of feeling, as if in reading poems we practiced emotion and understandings of emotion. Poetry by its bodily, mental, and emotional complex educates the sensibility, thinking and feeling appropriately melded together.

Words are to poems as stone to the stone-carving sculptor. When we say that we are parking the car we use the material of poetry; we do not speak it, any more than the contractor, spreading the parking lot's gravel, makes sculpture. Poetry is the only art that uses as its material something that everyone uses—and this commonness is both a strength of poetry and an impediment to reading it. *Poetry is not talk*. It sounds like talk—at least from

Wordsworth on, or even from Dante, it has been a commonplace that speech is our material—but poetry is talk altered into art, speech slowed down and attended to, words arranged for the reader who contracts to read them for their whole heft of associations and noises. If we try reading poetry with our eyes, as we learn to read newspapers, we miss its bodiliness as well as the history bodied into its words. Reading with care, so that a wholeness of language engages a wholeness of reading body and reading mind, we absorb poetry not with our eyes only nor with our ears at a poetry reading: We read with our mouths that chew on vowel and consonant; we read with our limbed muscles that enact the dance of the poem's rhythm; we read alert to the history and context of words. Robert Creeley's poem ends:

> Be for me, like rain,
> the getting out
>
> of the tiredness, the fatuousness, the semi-
> lust of intentional indifference.
> Be wet
> with a decent happiness.

When we read these lines with the slow attention we give Whitman or Hill, this rain sinks in.

All of us can ask directions or remark that it looks like snow. When we wish to embody in language a complex of feelings or sensations or ideas, we fall into inarticulateness; attempting to speak, in the heat of love or argument, we say nothing or we say what we do not intend. Poets encounter inarticulateness as much as anybody, or maybe more: They are aware of the word's inadequacy because they spend their lives struggling to say the unsayable. From time to time, in decades of devotion to their art, poets succeed in defeating the enemies of ignorance, deceit, and ugliness. The poets we honor most are those who—by studious imagination, by continuous connection to the sensuous body, and by spirit steeped in the practice and learning of language—say the unsayable.

MARVELL'S MANYNESS

During the question period they ask: "Who's your favorite poet?" When I was young and sophisticated I explained that I could not have one favorite; now I answer Thomas Hardy one day and Marianne Moore the next—or, more often than not, Andrew Marvell. Only Marvell would have made my short list forty-five years ago and all the years between. Of course the poetry has altered. Without a doubt he has produced, over the years of my growing up, much more work, most especially "An Horatian Ode upon Cromwell's Return from Ireland," which becomes available only when we have read a little history. "Upon Appleton House" eluded us when we were young and lazy because of its length; now its length is a luxury. It is also true that the range and import of the old poems has enlarged: Their scale has grown greater while their miniature size—pastoral conventions, carpe diem—has remained the same.

The analogy of scale and size comes from sculpture, which provides another analogy: When we look at a bronze or stone Henry Moore reclining figure, sited outdoors in a sculpture park, it changes every few inches as we walk around it. New lines-of-sight make new combinations, configurations, connections. If we continue to read a complex and multiple poem, as we grow older, it alters each time we return to it. The greater the poem the more it changes. We cannot read the same great poem twice. Thus "To His Coy Mistress" veers over the years from flesh to bone. Universality gathers upon "The Garden" as youth's gregariousness proves shallow, and as solitude enhances meditation or the pleasures of imagination. Conviction of historical ambiguity, or of human diversity within the ostensibly single self, illuminates and deepens "An Horatian Ode upon Cromwell's Return from Ireland."

We know about Andrew Marvell's life because of his politics, not because of his poetry. He was a lively controversialist during the Restoration, satirizing the court from his republican vantage. He was also the dutiful and assiduous Member of Parliament who represented the city of Hull. What we know of Marvell's life frustrates us, for the poet inside the Member remains elusive.

The poet's father, also Andrew Marvell, was born in Meldreth, eight miles south of Cambridge, educated at Emmanuel College, Cambridge, and in 1614 took the living at Winestead, in Holderness, where the poet was born seven years later. When Andrew *fils* was three years old, his father became preacher at Holy Trinity Church in Hull, as well as master of its grammar school; the poet was associated with the city for the rest of his life. (Three centuries later Philip Larkin lived and died there, librarian at the University.) Marvell's mother, whose name was Anne Pease, died in 1638, and his father remarried six months later—only to be drowned in 1640 while crossing the Humber. Thomas Fuller in his *Worthies*, who described the elder Marvell as "most facetious in his discourse, yet grave in his carriage," apportions blame: The preacher "drowned . . . by the carelessness (not to say drunkenness) of the boat-men." Apparently father and son suffered a contretemps a year before the father drowned. Scholars suggest that the poet left Trinity College, Cambridge (where he matriculated in 1633), in the company of Jesuits, a brief flirtation with the popery of which as satirist he became enemy. His father rooted him out of London—discovering him at a bookseller's—and brought him back to Trinity College and Puritan values.

When Marvell went down from Trinity he spent some years traveling on the continent, possibly as a tutor, during the onset of the civil wars. He left England in 1642 and returned probably in 1646, master of Dutch, Italian, French, and Spanish. Presumably his Latin and Greek were in place before he left. He wrote many Latin poems; at least one Greek poem survives. His Latin, both spoken and written, was fluent even for a seventeenth-century man of learning; he employed his languages in office under Cromwell and later on diplomatic missions during the Restoration.

Returned to England, he tutored Mary Fairfax, daughter of a Cromwellian general who had left the field, at Appleton House in Yorkshire from 1650 to 1653. There he probably wrote much of his best poetry. Later John Milton (Latin secretary to Cromwell; the office corresponded with foreign governments) recommended Marvell to Cromwell as tutor for a ward of the Lord Protector's living in Eton. Later still—in 1657—Marvell was appointed to assist Milton as Latin secretary. Another helper was the young John Dryden, many years later a Royalist antagonist of Andrew Marvell.

Marvell was first elected to Parliament in 1660. Like his father he was a moderate Puritan, Church of England; yet like many another Cromwellian, he welcomed the Restoration for stability's sake. Marvell used his relative political security to free Milton from jail; he may have saved Milton's life. Elected to Parliament, he served his constituents until his death. Many of his letters to the corporation of Hull are preserved in the Oxford University Press volumes of Marvell's *Poems and Letters*, meat for students of seventeenth-century English political life. These official letters frequently lament that taxes must be raised. Private notes to his nephew William Popple contain gossip and even scurrilous jokes about the king; but Marvell was no fervent anti-Royalist: He deplored courtly corruption but tolerated or perhaps indulged Charles the rake.

Marvell's political career was not without event. During his first Parliament he engaged in a public fistfight. From 1663 to 1665 he traveled on a trade embassy to Russia, with stops in Denmark and Sweden, an extraordinary adventure in the seventeenth century. Although we hear little about the journey in Marvell's own words, from other sources we understand that he was secretary to the mission and scripted letters home on behalf of the embassy's leader, the Earl of Carlisle. Czar Alexis professed dissatisfaction with Marvell's initial Latin address because Marvell called him Illustrissimus instead of Serenissimus. The embassy, which failed in its purpose, included a long series of aggravations. Early on, Marvell apparently pulled a gun on a recalcitrant teamster. On February 19, 1664, Czar Alexis provided his English visitors a banquet that lasted for nine hours and consisted of five hundred dishes. Marvell received the special attention of a sturgeon's head. We are told that the banquet ended early because the czar suffered a nosebleed.

In the last decade of his life, the public Marvell was quiet, representing Hull and reporting by regular letter to the corporation. Privately, or at any rate anonymously, Marvell was noisy: He occupied himself with political satire—anticourt, antipapist—in favor of toleration and liberty. When he died suddenly in 1678, perhaps of a stroke, it was rumored that Jesuits had poisoned him; he had recently satirized the Roman church.

Andrew Marvell never married. After his death his housekeeper Mary Palmer represented herself as Mary Marvell. (The poet's widow stood to receive some monies owed the poet's estate.) While he was alive, his political adversaries denounced Marvell as homosexual. Although his poems are full of pastoral love, no reader has ever discerned in his work tenderness toward a particular woman. The strongest erotic suggestion arises in "The Garden," where Marvell's vegetal eroticism exaggerates a convention. "The Definition of Love" can be read as an ironic description of the difficulties of homosexual love. Maybe it provides a rueful account of unfulfilled homoerotic desire:

> As lines so love oblique may well
> Themselves in every angle greet
> But ours so truly parallel
> Though infinite can never meet.

But we only speculate.

Of his politics we may say more. From the start Marvell was political. In the seventeenth century who could be apolitical? From time to time he appears to stand on both sides of a question: His attack on the Cromwellian Tom May was written during Cromwell's time—when he also wrote Cromwellian panegyrics. At the same time one may discern consistencies in Marvell: He favored religious toleration, whether its opponents were low church or high; he attacked corruption in the Long Parliament—and again in the court of Charles II. Stories are told of Marvell's incorruptibility, of his refusal to take a bribe. If he seems at times "to stand on both sides of a question," we must ask how many issues limited themselves to two sides. The seventeenth century was politically many-sided, more complex than our own age, and one need not have been the Vicar of Bray to appear inconsistent. To divide England into parties of Cavalier and Roundhead is to preclude understanding. One could stand to the Parliament side on a dozen issues, and to the Court side on a dozen others—at the same time, without inconsistency, much less hypocrisy.

Mixed loyalties were standard. Some rebels of the Long Parliament considered themselves loyal subjects who wished to save the king from wicked advisers. (Decapitation seems an extreme measure of correction.) Take Marvell's employer Fairfax, a great general for Cromwell against the king. (Milton addressed a sonnet to the parliamentary hero, "To My Lord Fairfax," "whose name in arms through Europe rings.") Fairfax resigned his command when he disagreed with the Lord Protector;

a Presbyterian himself, he would not invade Scotland. His wife was aghast at the execution of Charles I; it was rumored that My Lord Fairfax shared her opinion. Retired from combat, Fairfax returned to his country seat in Yorkshire, and later corresponded with Charles II from Appleton House. This old Cromwellian general helped to restore Charles II in 1660.

Ambivalence wove its texture into details of all private and practical arrangements. The boy whom Marvell had tutored at Eton—Cromwell's ward William Dutton—was son of a Cavalier who died in 1646 in the Royalist forces, but whose uncle arranged that William marry Cromwell's youngest daughter. Of course, when ambivalence tries to act, it finds itself incapable. That Cromwell's ward was Royalist did not keep the king's head on his shoulders. To take part in the life of their times, Fairfax or Marvell or Milton needed perforce to take sides. From time to time, throughout his life, Marvell in his satires could sound dogmatic and singleminded. Only when he writes great poetry does Marvell's language embody ambivalence or manyness. If ambivalence makes for paralyzed politics and anarchic governance, it makes for poetry complex enough to mimic human complexity; in Marvell, it made for great poetry.

It is a mark of Marvell's honorable manyness that, if he had published the "Horatian Ode" in his lifetime, he would have been in trouble with both regicide and loyalist. He published little in his lifetime—poems printed in anthologies—and none of the poems for which we honor him. After his death, in 1681, his nephew William Popple issued *Miscellaneous Poems*. Only in small measure may we attribute this absence of publication to politics. Marvell was not a professional poet, as the young John Dryden was. Marvell's attitude toward himself as a poet is old-fashioned: he resembles not Ben Jonson but Sir Walter Raleigh, or his own contemporary John Wilmot, Earl of Rochester, who was poet among his other roles—gentleman and rake, for instance. Marvell was a poet while he was tutor, Latinist, bureaucrat, and M.P.

Marvell was also old-fashioned in poetic style, which helps to account for the strange history of his reputation. Usually he hoed his tetrameter garden, instead of going avant-garde with the heroic couplet that Dryden spent his life exploring and extending. Marvell also cultivated the old metaphoric extravagance associated with John Donne, the out-of-fashion, faintly fusty metaphysical style. To someone reading his work late in the seventeenth century, Marvell must have seemed reactionary—like Thomas Hardy writing rhymed lyrics in the heyday of 1920s modernism.

When Popple published *Miscellaneous Poems*, no one celebrated a great poet. For that matter readers lacked Marvell's greatest work: "An Horatian Ode" was suppressed until a century after his death. (Popple at first seems to have included it: This poem and the lesser verses on Cromwell's death turn up in two surviving copies; in all other copies they have been removed.) It was not until 1776 that Marvell's Cromwellian poems reached print to remain there.

Meanwhile Marvell the lyric poet lacked an audience. When English booksellers picked the poets for Samuel Johnson to write about, in *Lives of the Poets*, Marvell's name went unlisted: At the time, his name would not have occurred to anyone. Other seventeenth-century poets, like Robert Herrick and Thomas Campion, also remained forgotten until the Romantics found them, but Marvell had the misfortune to be remembered for something other than his poetry. All through the eighteenth century, his was a name to conjure with, for Whigs and lovers of liberty. Jonathan Swift praised and learned from Marvell's satirical prose, especially *The Rehearsal Transpros'd*. When Wordsworth thought of Marvell it was as a son of liberty: "Great men have been among us . . . Sydney, Marvell, Harrington."

It took a later generation of Romantics to discover the poetry. At first they considered him merely a poet of nature, but once he was reprinted, the limits of this discovery could expand. The antiquarian Charles Lamb found him, read him, and praised him. William Hazlitt reprinted some of the best work in an 1825 collection. Palgrave treasury'd him. Tennyson recited him to friends. Ward in *English Poets* (1880) left out "To His Coy Mistress" (perhaps as distressing in 1880 as praise for Cromwell in 1681) but included "An Horatian Ode," "The Bermudas," and "The Garden."

One would think the battle won. But, if we had learned to admire the poetry, we had not credited its greatness. When Augustine Birrell wrote about Marvell in 1905, for the *English Men of Letters* series, he was modest or scrupulous to limit his praise. "A finished master of his art," Birrell says, "he never was." He compares Marvell's skill unfavorably with the poetry of Lovelace, Cowley, and Waller. "He is often clumsy," Birrell writes, "and sometimes almost babyish."

In 1922 the Oxford University Press published *Andrew Marvell*, tercentenary tributes by eight critics including mossbacks like Edmund Gosse and J. C. Squire—and the young turk T. S. Eliot. We consult this volume to read the Tercentenary Sermon at Holy Trinity Church and the Tercentenary Address at the Guild Hall in Hull, or to read about "The Marvell Tramcars" and study photographs of a Hull trolley repainted in honor of the city's poet and parliamentarian. But it was Eliot's great essay, reprinted from the *Times Literary Supplement*, which especially fixed our attention on Marvell's excellence: After being neglected for two centuries, and condescended to for another, he was at last discovered.

When you love a poet's poems, it is annoying to feel required to adduce reasons. But if you are to move a skeptic you need to try. For at least a hundred years people have used

> Annihilating all that's made
> To a green thought in a green shade

as an example of poetry or even the poetic. In the seventeenth century this couplet would have been an example of wit; by history's revisionary magic two centuries later its wit vanished in romantic smoke. Its thoughtful trope—an exaggeration of concentration, the inward defining itself as outward—came to seem mystic: a moment of pantheistic ego-loss or Freud's oceanic feeling. Why not both at once?

Surely this couplet is poetry at its most condensed. Marvell was expert at loading every rift with ore. Rift-and-ore is never mere quantity, more midgets in the Volkswagen; rifts are most ore'd when number is not so much dense as various. The smoothly rolling polysyllabic Latin of *Annihilating*, with its densely syntax'd accusative English monosyllabic *all that's made*, contrasts with (and completes itself in) a monosyllabic line absolutely balanced—preposition / article / adjective / noun, preposition / article / adjective / noun—in which four out of eight monosyllables appear twice. Wit and grammar together serve to embody a pleasurable and mildly scary vaguening of consciousness: both at once. Three hundred years of consciousness about consciousness hook together in these lines.

Marvell's banner reads: *Both at Once*. The simultaneous affirmation of opposing forces—by no means limited to two items—requires compression. By this compression we not only acknowledge ambivalence, we embody it.

His couplets accommodate a vast range of tone and of pacing. If the beginning of "To His Coy Mistress" is old-fashioned and metaphysical—hyperbolic-witty, slow in its performance of slowness—the end of the poem is modern, streamlined, and speeds like nothing else in English poetry: and all, perforce, to the same octosyllabic tune. Barbara Everett alludes to the "Horatian Ode" when she observes that "Marvell is using a metre for thinking aloud in"—but in his great poems he always uses meter to think aloud in. The tetrameter couplet balanced four against four, and each four balanced two against two—except when enjambment and eccentric caesura saw that it didn't, which was shocking or outrageous:

> Thus though we cannot make our sun
> Stand still, yet we will make him run.

Poetry is a language for thinking aloud in—and not for putting thoughts into words, although the philosophical heresy is almost universal among critics. (Everett provides an exception.) Metaphor, syntax, image, meter, and rhythm are means-of-thought; so is overall construction. "To His Coy Mistress" has been well observed: its logical structure, its combinations of flesh and bone, time and space, eros and thanatos, its use of poetic conventions two thousand years old. It is a culminating poem in a millennial sequence that affirms: *Make love because you die*. In the process this theme combines in one poem the two subjects of human discourse: *both at once*.

Poetry exists, not only Marvell's, to say and do *both at once*. Philosophical discourse dedicates itself to find, to set forth, and to decide what's first or best or true. Only poetry admits (proclaims, insists, shouts): *both at once!* or even *all at once!* (Therefore I need call Heraclitus, Emerson, and Nietzsche poets.) Surely Marvell is foremost among the manysayers. Manyness is ineluctably human, and poetry (among human artifacts) best embodies manyness.

Although we need from time to time to make a choice—Marvell voted, Marvell advocated and denounced—choices are always *faute de mieux*. To pretend otherwise is to lie, an activity deplored by the Muse. Utterly captured by the mixed political life of seventeenth-century England, housed with many-sided Fairfax at Nun Appleton, Marvell found in the expression of ambivalence his poetic form and power.

If Marvell made the octosyllabic couplet his own, using the modern pentameter couplet only for lighter work, he experimented in his greatest single work to marry the tetrameter couplet to a trimeter, constructing the eloquent, heartbreaking stanza of the "Horatian Ode." The Cromwell who appears in Marvell's poem is massive, violent, and willful:

> Then burning through the air he went,
> And palaces and temples rent:
> > And Caesar's head at last
> > Did through his laurels blast.

The last line trembles the scale, as we sort its syntax out and watch "blast" perform its possibilities. We must reconstruct Marvell's Cromwell away from normative leaders like Napoleon and Hitler, who have been praised in similar terms, because on the other hand, "Much to the man is due . . ."

> Who, from his private gardens, where
> He lived reserved and austere,
> > As if his highest plot
> > To plant the bergamot,
>
> Could by industrious valour climb
> To ruin the great work of time,
> > And cast the kingdoms old
> > Into another mould.

Meter, consonants, and syntax mimic strength, embody phallic masculine muscularity and determination. In the great couplet, "Could by industrious valour climb / To ruin the great work of time," Marvell clearly values both "valour" and "the great work." Emotions conflict, values conflict, and "valour" destroys "great work" as an army lays waste to a castle. I think of Yeats's oxymoron, "terrible beauty," in "Easter, 1916"—where "is born" gives narrow victory to beauty over terror.

Marvell the traditionalist poet is not unmoved by tradition. The poem continues directly:

> Though justice against fate complain,
> And plead the ancient rights in vain:
>> But those do hold or break
>> As men are strong or weak.
> Nature, that hateth emptiness,
> Allows of penetration less:
>> And therefore must make room
>> Where greater spirits come.

The most eloquent and touching stanzas describe the execution of Charles, written by the poet later described by Royalists as a "bitter Republican."

> He nothing common did or mean
> Upon that memorable scene:
>> But with his keener eye
>> The axe's edge did try:
> Nor called the gods with vulgar spite
> To vindicate his helpless right,
>> But bowed his comely head,
>> Down, as upon a bed.

Everett remarks "Everything is beautiful, and something is betrayed." There's nothing greater in English poetry than this beautiful betrayal—but Marvell does not end with this passage that would have ended most poets' poems. Praise for Cromwell continues to find glory in the power, and yet the poem ends in the prophetic aside that shades itself back over the hundred and eighteen lines before.

> The same arts that did gain
> A power, must it maintain.

The poise of Marvell's judgment wavers, but it concludes, as it does in his great poems, with an appropriately complex justice. Such conclusions are neither simple nor comforting—except that the existence of honest, difficult, human intelligence consoles us: Poetry's thinking consoles us.

LONG ROBINSON

In 1869, Edwin Arlington Robinson was born in the village of Head Tide in Maine, third son and final child of Edward and Mary Robinson; his brothers Dean and Herman were twelve and four. Because his mother had wanted a daughter, Robinson began life as a disappointment; he went unnamed for half a year. When a summer visitor insisted that the six-month-old baby be named, "Edwin" was chosen by lot; the poet's middle name remembered the provenance of the visitor. As he grew up in Gardiner, where the family moved shortly after his birth, this poet of failure and defeat was known as "Win"; he preferred "Long Robinson" himself—at six-foot-two, he was tall for his generation—but his friends later settled for "E.A.R.," which was appropriate enough: The near anonymity of initials fitted the shadowy silence of his character; and he had a beautiful ear.

Perhaps because she never welcomed him, Robinson doted on his mother. His father prospered while the Union did—store-keeper, small-time banker, investor—and favored his second son Herman, businessman and entrepreneur. Robinson loathed

Herman (not coincidentally, he adored Herman's wife Emma) while he admired his elder brother Dean, who became a doctor. Then the family fell apart in a rapid series of disasters: Dean became addicted to morphine; the 1893 panic destroyed Herman's fortunes and Edward's investments in Herman's schemes; Edward took to drink and died; not much later, Mary died of diphtheria. Remnants of the Robinson fortune bought a Gardiner drugstore, at least partly as a source for Dean's morphine. Then Dean died, probably by deliberate overdose, and Herman turned alcoholic, hawking lobsters in Gardiner's streets while Emma took in sewing. Later, Herman died in the public ward of a Massachusetts hospital.

E.A.R. never took a college degree; but to graduate from a good high school in the 1890s was to know history and languages. He made close friends at Harvard, where he spent two years as a special student, and where he first published in undergraduate magazines. He studied philosophy, English literature, and languages—without distinquishing himself unduly—but Harvard was his entry into a larger world, his release from provincialism; he indulged himself happily in bibulous Cambridge talk. Robinson loved cities; all his life, he doted on theatre, opera, and orchestral music.

By his mid-twenties the character had emerged that endured until death. E.A.R. refused with few exceptions to hold down a job or work for a living. He was "a confirmed bachelor," as the cliche has it, with a calling for solitude; the phrase was not a euphemism for homosexuality. Like other males of his time, Robinson presumably sought professional relief when he was young—he wrote poems about prostitutes—but his erotic experience was probably limited. A frequently repeated story has him rejecting an offer from Isadora Duncan. Some of his friends in their reminiscences hint at love affairs; certainly he cherished unacceptable love for his brother's wife and widow. It is clear that several times in his life he thought about marriage, especially to the beautiful Emma after Herman's death; but we may doubt that he came close.

E.A.R. was affectionate, as his letters show, but in person he was shy and often dumb. Many anecdotes illustrate his silence, or immense silences terminated by monosyllables. Only late at night, after considerable whiskey, did Robinson become voluble; if he was an alcoholic, like his father and brother, surely his drinking began as self-medication for shyness, melancholy, and silence. When he finally found readers, when summers at the MacDowell Colony added structure and society to his year, he stopped drinking—only to resume later in response to the Volstead Act, which he considered "fundamentally evil and arbitrary."

When he was not married to whiskey he was married to art. If he read Yeats's poem about choosing perfection of the life or of the work, he never doubted the choice. He wrote in a letter, "Do you know I have a theory that Browning's life-long happiness with his wife is all humbug? The man's life was in his art." Maybe his concentration on the art of poetry compensated for love's loss: his mother's; Emma's. Whatever its irrational source, his devotion to making poetry remained fundamental. All his life, he characterized himself as someone who could do only one thing.

In Gardiner after he had graduated from high school, staying at home except for his two years at Harvard, he lived with his family as a sort of servant or hired man, tending the garden and doing odd jobs, working at his poetry as he could. After his mother died he moved to fin-de-siècle New York. For twenty years he survived on a tiny inheritance, on the charity of others, and on free lunches in saloons; he turned down the journalistic opportunities that largely supported rival poets. He labored for a while as timekeeper for workers constructing the subway. Back in Massachusetts, he failed as an office boy at Harvard. Returned to New York he continued the old Bohemian life of furnished rooms and patched clothing. "I starved twenty years," he said late in life, "and in my opinion no one should write poetry unless he is willing to starve for it." Once he laboriously accumulated nickels toward a new pair of trousers, then plunged his savings into a Metropolitan Opera ticket for *Tristan und Isolde*. Continually he worked at his verses, sitting in a rocking chair in a bare room high over a New York street, solitary and industrious, revising his lines over and over again. On several occasions he worked on stories and plays, trying to earn a living with his pen, but failed utterly. He was right, however much he fulfilled his own prophecy: Poetry was the one thing he could do.

Which made it a pity that no one thought he could do it.

E.A.R. published his first book at his own expense in 1896: He mailed out many copies, receiving letters of praise but no significant attention. His second and third books—many essential poems derive from the early volumes—appeared because of subsidies or guarantees from more affluent friends. Magazine editors rejected his best work—at a time when many magazines printed poems, or what passed for poems—because they were realistic. (Robinson admired Zola; remember that he wrote at a time when *Jude* was obscene.) In the 1890s and the 1900s, magazine poems told cheerful lies in words considered pretty: As Robinson bragged of his first book (1896), "there is not a red-bellied robin in the whole collection." It was daring, shocking, and unacceptable to write sonnets about butchers overcome with grief or about hired men who spoke the common language. After a decade of assiduous labor and continual discouragement, Robinson sank into alcoholic depression. "For seven years," he told a friend late in his life, over a tumbler of whiskey, "I had *ab-so-lute-ly* nothing but the bottle." His friend reports that E.A.R. loved to say "*ab-so-lute-ly*."

Then, early in the century, before the Great War, several things happened almost at once. The first event was most astonishing—the arrival of a letter with a White House frank. Theodore Roosevelt's son Kermit attended Groton, where an English master from Gardiner, Maine, showed him the unknown poet's poems; impressed, Kermit showed the book to his father in the White House—who was dazzled, and who found Robinson in New York and offered to help: Would the poet take a consular position in Mexico or Canada? Robinson settled for a sinecure in Customs in New York—he loved New York—which allowed him to help Herman's widow and daughters when they needed it. T.R. then bullied his own publisher into reissuing a Robinson volume and reviewed Robinson's poems from the presidential desk; of course, opposition newspapers ridiculed the incumbent's taste.

Two further miracles were required. First was the MacDowell Colony in Peterborough, New Hampshire—just beginning—which E.A.R. visited reluctantly and was amazed to enjoy. MacDowell provided a structure for the remainder of his structureless life; every summer from 1911 on E.A.R. rocking-chaired in a MacDowell studio. He visited Massachusetts friends in spring and fall, and spent his winters in New York, but Peterborough was the frame for his year's house. For most colonists, MacDowell is a release from family life into creative solitude; for E.A.R. the colony *was* family life. He sat in his own chair for dinner, indulging his "idiom of silence," as a friend called it, among a knot of artists year after year.

The third miracle was the gradual emergence of an American literary and artistic culture or community, of which MacDowell itself was a sign. America had already produced great artists, but some had lived much of the time in Europe; some had been learned and provincial in Massachusetts (Emerson, Longfellow, Thoreau, Hawthorne); and some had been the magnificent eccentrics (Whitman, Dickinson, Melville) who were our greatest writers—masters or mistresses of separation, who lived at the brilliant margin of the national life.

Then, in 1912, Harriet Monroe started *Poetry* in Chicago (poetry in *Chicago!*) and Ezra Pound corresponding from London supplied her with T. S. Eliot, H. D. Imagiste—and Robert Frost. Pound, Eliot, and H. D. still required Europe but now *Poetry* (also: *Broom*; *Secession*; *The Dial*; *Others*; *The Little Re-*

view; also: the Armory Show; Stieglitz) and its ambience rendered the United States possible for poets who worked in a community, like most artists over history. Wallace Stevens, Marianne Moore, and William Carlos Williams did not need to carry their sensibilities to England or France or Italy. Instead, they argued about linebreaks and Marcel Duchamp at weekend picnics in New Jersey.

When E.A.R. finally turned famous, the monthlies that had rejected him for decades started to court him (the way the *Atlantic*, played like a fiddle by Robert Frost, printed Frost poems that they had earlier rejected). E.A.R.'s personal fortunes began to improve when he was fifty: prizes, honorary degrees, and money (*Tristram* sold almost sixty thousand copies its first year). The old Bohemian, with indecent speed, became a figure of respectable eminence. It is seldom observed that E.A.R. also published in *Poetry*—with Eliot's "The Love Song of J. Alfred Prufrock," with Pound and Stevens and Moore. In one issue— March 1914—Harriet Monroe published Carl Sandburg's most famous poem "Chicago" ("Hog butcher to the world," etc.) and the poem "Eros Turannos," which is arguably Robinson's best.

"Eros Turannos" tells about a marriage, in a Maine coastal town, between a fortune hunter and a woman of old family who marries to avoid solitary old age. Robinson catches the man's opportunism and the woman's desperation.

> She fears him, and will always ask
> What fated her to choose him;
> She meets in his engaging mask
> All reasons to refuse him;

But what she meets and what she fears
Are less than are the downward years,
Drawn slowly to the foamless weirs
    Of age, were she to lose him.

A sense of ocean and old trees
    Envelops and allures him;
Tradition, touching all he sees,
    Beguiles and reassures him;
And all her doubts of what he says
Are dimmed with what she knows of days—
Till even prejudice delays
    And fades, and she secures him.

It does not take long before she understands her error; she se-
cludes herself while townspeople gossip about her eccentricity
or madness:

The falling leaf inaugurates
    The reign of her confusion;
The pounding wave reverberates
    The dirge of her illusion;
And home, where passion lived and died,
Becomes a place where she can hide,
While all the town and harbor side
    Vibrate with her seclusion.

There follows a stanza of padding and needless qualification.
Such wasted motion often annoys us in Robinson; we learn to
scan such passages quickly, bored but anticipatory, to reach his
constructed conclusion:

Meanwhile we do no harm; for they
    That with a god have striven,
Not hearing much of what we say,
    Take what the god has given;
Though like waves breaking it may be,

> Or like a changed familiar tree,
> Or like a stairway to the sea
>   Where down the blind are driven.

The first four lines reaffirm the title: Her struggle, not with a secular king but with a divine tyrant, achieves nothing but madness and dysphoria.

Robinson tells his story in a stanza form that might seem fitted to light verse. (Yvor Winters noted that Robinson's prosody borrows from W. M. Praed's.) He constructs his stanza out of a quatrain made of tetrameters and trimeters, the B-rhymes double, followed by a tetrameter tercet and concluded by a trimeter, the last line double-rhyming with lines two and four. How can such a jingle render feeling?

Here's how: His similes are structural, not decorative, as "like waves breaking" embodies the relentless dolor of a featureless daily life; as "like a changed familiar tree" alludes to the "family tree" and combines ancestral pride with debasement; as "like a stairway to the sea" foreshadows inevitable descent into death, recalls the "foamless weirs / Of age," and suggests possible suicide by drowning—tyrannical Love driving its victim into the sea. These similes conclude the poem with a passage that is tragic, ironic—and gorgeous.

But it cannot be ironic in its metrical form—or gorgeous in its compressed and witty style—unless the reader's ear is conditioned by the glorious tradition of meter in English: another reason for the diminishment of this poet's reputation.

Although he wrote creditable book-length poems in blank verse, the best of Robinson's poems are rhymed and brief.

Among his best shorter narratives is "Isaac and Archibald," a wonderful poem in a blank verse derived (like Frost's) from Wordsworth; slightly less valuable are "Ben Jonson Entertains a Man from Stratford" and "Rembrandt to Rembrandt." For glories in a more Tennysonian blank verse, the reader may look at the lush conclusions to the book-length poems *Merlin* and *Tristram*.

A few fine lyrics describe the natural world, existing for their own sweet sakes, for the joy or ecstasy of their saying or singing:

> Dark hills at evening in the west,
> Where sunset hovers like a sound
> Of golden horns that sang to rest
> Old bones of warriors under ground,
> Far now from all the bannered ways
> Where flash the legions of the sun,
> You fade—as if the last of days
> Were fading, and all wars were done.

"The Dark Hills" compares landscape to romance, and Robinson is more moved by Roman legionaries or King Arthur than by Mount Monadnock.

Usually, by Heraclitean paradox, the man of silence and solitude wrote poems about people, poems of character and story. His narrative sonnets provide a characteristic signature: usually a bizarre or extraordinary story. A prostitute's sonnet ("The Growth of 'Lorraine'") ends: "'I'm going to the devil.'—And she went." We read of a dying blind man ("Ben Trovato") whose mistress has fled, whose wife wears the mistress's fur so that he will die mistaken (and content) over whose hand he holds. Again and again we read of suicide ("The Mill") and failure, of business as greed and ruin, of capitulation to twin devils of drugs and alcohol. Or we read of the butcher's grief:

Reuben Bright

Because he was a butcher and thereby
Did earn an honest living (and did right),
I would not have you think that Reuben Bright
Was any more a brute than you or I;
For when they told him that his wife must die,
He stared at them, and shook with grief and fright,
And cried like a great baby half that night,
And made the women cry to see him cry.

And after she was dead, and he had paid
The singers and the sexton and the rest,
He packed a lot of things that she had made
Most mournfully away in an old chest
Of hers, and put some chopped-up cedar boughs
In with them, and tore down the slaughter-house.

Robinson's octave ends with wild grief; but the active imagination of the sestet is his genius—the cow-killer converted. This sonnet's beauty is not diminished by an anecdote: In its initial printing, a magnificent proof hack changed the last phrase to: "tore down to the slaughter house."

For other narratives of character read *passim*, not forgetting early work; "Luke Havergal," from the Harvard years, captivated T.R. Few of his philosophical poems succeed: "The Man Against the Sky" and "Octaves" do not think so well; an exception is "Hillcrest," dour and fierce, relentlessly intelligent:

Who sees unchastened here the soul
Triumphant has no other sight

> Than has a child who sees the whole
> World radiant with his own delight.
>
> Far journeys and hard wandering
> Await him in whose crude surmise
> Peace, like a mask, hides everything
> That is and has been from his eyes;
>
> And all his wisdom is unfound,
> Or like a web that error weaves
> On airy looms that have a sound
> No louder now than falling leaves.

The best work remains anecdotal and ethical, like "The Poor Relation," "Isaac and Archibald," "Eros Turannos," and—why not?—"Mr. Flood's Party," which is funny and miserable with an appropriate misery. With a subject—loneliness in old age— suggesting sentimentality, Robinson mocks himself and his old man by an overreaching reference to Roland's horn, and by a triple-switch that goes the necessary step beyond expectation: He sets us up with a sentimental simile—

> Then, as a mother lays her sleeping child
> Down tenderly, fearing it may awake,

and then swoops the chair from beneath our descendant backsides—

> He set the jug down slowly at his feet
> With trembling care,

so that, with a gross vaudeville humor, we laugh at the joke— his baby is the jug!—until Robinson takes genius's third step:

> knowing that most things break.

This lesson Robinson knew from his family and Gardiner, Maine.

If we are old enough, we grew up learning that modern poetry *has* to be difficult; therefore, "Mr. Flood's Party" cannot be modern poetry, or maybe (by idiotic extension) poetry at all. According to this requirement, neither Frost nor Hardy can be poets either—and indeed I remember the 1940s when the poems of Frost and Hardy were inadmissible or at least embarrassing and awkward of admission. By the end of this century, we have brought Hardy and Frost back without (let me hope) needing to expel Eliot, Stevens, Moore, Williams, and Pound.

We must bring Robinson back. Although he remains among the best American poets, Robinson now goes largely unread. An insidious form of neglect enshrines one minor effort, genuflects, and bypasses the best work. Robinson is remembered chiefly for a brief story in quatrains, punchy as a television ad, in which the protagonist surprises us (once) by putting a bullet through his head.

Robinson was the poet chosen as sacrifice to modernism. The poetic enemy, addressed at the turn of the century by the young T. S. Eliot and Ezra Pound, was someone like Richard Watson Gilder—not Robinson—but by the 1930s no one knew Gilder's name; and Robinson was momentarily notorious for multiple Pulitzers and for writing a best-selling blank verse Arthurian narrative. When he was young Robinson sounded like no one else—and paid the price; but to the unhistoric ear of a later era, Robinson's poetry, when set beside "The Waste

Land," sounded Victorian. If the combative Eliot needed to dismiss Robinson as "negligible," it is understandable. But surely we need no longer dismiss the author of "Eros Turranos" and "Isaac and Archibald" because he wrote iambics in a coherent syntax.

The generation of great poets, after the magnificent solitaries Dickinson and Whitman, begins with Robinson and Frost before it moves to Pound, Stevens, Moore, and Eliot. Robinson was essential to this motion, in his realism or honesty, and in his relentless care for the art of poetic language. Reading his letters or his sparse table-talk, one encounters his dour, unforgiving professionalism. Woe to the friend who counts "fire" as two syllables or who heaps one preposition on top of another.

Robinson was master of verse and poetry, of metric and diction, syntax and tone, rhyme and understanding, ethics, metaphor, and the exposure of greed. The last nouns in this series are not disconnected from the first: Dead metaphors are unethical, and forced rhymes are corrupt. In monkish solitude, with painstaking and moral attention, in long hours of revision, he made great poems. Once at MacDowell, at an evening meal, he was outraged to hear someone boast of having written hundreds of lines that day. Speaking slowly, or stingily, he told how he had spent four hours in the morning placing a hyphen between two words—and four hours in the afternoon taking it out.

LAMENT FOR A MAKER

I that in heill wes and gladnes,
Am trublit now with gret seiknes,
And feblit with infermitie;
   Timor mortis conturbat me.

He hes done petuously devour
The noble Chaucer, of makaris flowr,
The Monk of Bery, and Gower, all thre;
   Timor mortis conturbat me.

He hes Blind Hary and Sandy Traill
Slaine with his schour of mortall haill,
Quhilk Patrik Johnestoun might nocht fle;
   Timor mortis conturbat me.

—WILLIAM DUNBAR,
FROM "LAMENT FOR THE MAKARIS"

It is a mystery, how poetry will thrive in an age or a country, then fade out only to appear elsewhere. Between Chaucer (dead in 1400) and Wyatt (born in 1503), poetry was sparse in England and copious north of the border in William Dunbar's Scotland. When he lamented the dead and dying poets, William Dunbar listed "The noble Chaucer, of poets the flower, / The Monk of Bery, and Gower, all three. / *Timor mortis conturbat me.*" (The fear of death confounds me.) Gower died just after

Chaucer, and Lydgate in a Bury St. Edmunds monastery half a century later. Mostly, Dunbar mourns the Scots makers, naming twenty-five dead and dying poets in twenty-five stanzas; of most of the poets he names, not a line survives. When Dunbar complains that "Gud Maister Walter Kennedy / In point of dede lyes veraly. / Gret reuth it wer that so sould be. / *Timor mortis conturbat me*," he must speak of a dear friend, for "The Flyting of Dunbar and Kennedie" survives. (A flyting is a poets' fight or slanging match.) In another stanza, Dunbar mourns the genius of his age, author of "The Testament of Cresseid" which is the great work between Chaucer and Shakespeare: "In Dumfermline he hes done roune / With Maister Robert Henrysoun."

Dunbar's "Lament" is a universal elegy for the dead poets. James Wright, who loved it, recited this poem in my hearing half a dozen times, in what passed with us for a Scots accent; his mouth relished the names: "Blind Harry," "Sandy Traill," "Sir Mungo Lockhart of the Lee." Jim died in 1980 and many friends have lamented this maker; has any American poet been subject to so many elegies? He was born (Martins Ferry, Ohio) on 13 December 1927, and belonged like Dunbar to a numerous and varied generation of poets—makers of James Wright's moment—and this poetic community of friends and rivals was central to his life and work.* We were aware of each other. At

---

*Also born in 1927 were John Ashbery, Galway Kinnell, and W. S. Merwin. Maybe 1926 was the annus mirabilis—Robert Bly, Robert Creeley, Allen Ginsberg, James Merrill, Frank O'Hara, A. R. Ammons, W. D. Snodgrass, David Wagoner—unless it was 1923: Denise Levertov, James Dickey, Richard Hugo, James Schuyler, Anthony Hecht, Alan Dugan, John Logan, Louis Simpson. There was also 1924: John Haines, Jane Cooper, Edgar Bowers;

Harvard College I argued poetry with Bly, Rich, Creeley, O'Hara, Ashbery, and Koch; at the same time Merwin and Kinnell read Yeats at Princeton; Louis Simpson returned from the war to the Columbia of Allen Ginsberg, where the young would soon include Hollander and Howard. Wright studied under John Crowe Ransom at Kenyon College, overlapping with Robert Mezey and the novelist E. L. Doctorow. Philip Whalen and Gary Snyder roomed together at Reed College. A little later, Iowa collected Philip Levine, Donald Justice, and W. D. Snodgrass. Never had so many American poets crowded into one decade to be born. Then in 1966 Frank O'Hara died of injuries suffered in an accident; Paul Blackburn died in 1971, Anne Sexton in 1974, L. E. Sissman in 1976, James Wright in 1980, Richard Hugo in 1982, and John Logan in 1987. *Timor mortis* . . .

Why were so many poets born in the 1920s? This generation emerged blinking into the American Century—which lasted from 1945 to 1963—as the first literary generation in American history for whom Europe was not an issue. (James Wright's love of Italy and France implied no diffidence about American poetry. His love was the northerner's discovery of sun and flesh; he burrowed in the sweet meat of the Italian pear.) This generation grew up alienated adolescents in milltowns and suburbs, in Cal-

---

1925: Donald Justice, Gerald Stern, Carolyn Kizer, Maxine Kumin, Philip Booth, Kenneth Koch; 1928: Philip Levine, Anne Sexton, L. E. Sissman, Peter Davison, me; 1929: Adrienne Rich, X. J. Kennedy, Ed Dorn, John Hollander, Richard Howard; 1930: Gary Snyder, Gregory Corso. In 1931 came Etheridge Knight, in 1932 Sylvia Plath—but as we stray outside the decade, the numbers diminish.

ifornia, on the great plains, in factory cities, and in Palm Beach. Like all generations of American artists, this generation was largely middle class—but these childhoods endured the Depression. In Martins Ferry, across the river from West Virginia, James Wright's father Dudley worked in the Hazel-Atlas Glass factory all his life, laid off during bad times. Although Jim admired and praised his father—who never surrendered to adversity—the family lived through hardships, enduring the 1930s under threat of poverty in a succession of rented houses. Jim's whole life was compelled by his necessity to leave the blighted valley, to escape his father's fate—and *never* to work at Hazel-Atlas Glass. In his poems, Martins Ferry and its sibling valley towns blacken with Satanic mills along the river and under the green hill.

When he graduated from high school and joined the Army at eighteen, he planned to avoid the factories by means of the G.I. Bill and a college education. Once he wrote me about his Army paydays in Japan: "I was paid $120. on the first day of each month. And I remember walking, every single time, from the end of the payline to the Fort post office, two blocks away, and writing a money order for exactly $110 . . . sending it home to Ohio for banking . . . At the time I thought of nothing but the Ohio Valley (i.e., death, real death of soul) on the one side and life (escape to my own life . . .) on the other." For no one more than James Wright was literature so much the choice of life over death: Thomas Hardy and Beethoven on the one hand; on the other hand Martins Ferry and Hazel-Atlas Glass. "Life" was *art*, poetry as paradise or at least as refuge—for the free and natural expression of feeling, for delight in the wit and sensuousness of words, and for sensitivity or receptivity to the world's pleasures. At the same time, most importantly for James Wright, poetry expressed and enacted compassion over the world's suffering.

He was fifteen when he started to write his poems. Words in the mouth must have pleased him always; when you heard Jim tell a story, or say a poem, you felt his joy in saying the words, the words in his mouth. There was also for Jim the desire to make in art an alternative and improved universe. If he reviled his Ohio, he understood that Ohio made him; and he understood that Ohio remained his material. We choose exile as a vantage point; from exile we look back on the rejected, rejecting place—to make our poems both out of it *and* against it. Wright's poems, alternatives to Ohio, are populated with people who never left the valley—factory workers and fullbacks, executed murderers, drunks, and down-and-outs. If some of his *maudits* derive from other milieux—from the Pacific Northwest, from Minneapolis, from New York—they live the life Jim intended to abandon by leaving the Ohio Valley. Withdrawing from his desolate internal Ohio, he observed and preserved. He is like Yeats's musician in "Lapis Lazuli," privileged to observe the "tragic scene" and to make, with the skill of his "accomplished fingers," "mournful melodies."

The "mournful" began early on the fifty-two-year journey. In 1943, when he turned sixteen, Jim lost a year of high school to a nervous breakdown. There would be more breakdowns—but he struggled against breakage, as later with the branch inclined to break, and graduated from high school. When he mustered out of the Army in 1947, he entered Kenyon College—the most literary enclave in the state of Ohio, with its poet Ransom, its tradition of student-writers, and the *Kenyon Review*, which was the journal of its national literary moment. Older than his classmates, he would graduate at twenty-three in January 1952. Attending Kenyon, Jim must have felt at home for the first time in his life—among teachers like Charles Coffin and Philip Timberlake as well as Ransom; and with literary and even writerly friends among the undergraduates. At the same time, he must have felt the scholarship boy's guilt, living for the first time among people largely middle class. It could not have been easy, and his G.I. Bill ran out after his junior year. Jim used his brain to keep himself at Kenyon and later to study abroad and to send himself to graduate school. When he made Phi Beta Kappa as a junior, Kenyon gave him a full scholarship for his senior year.

As an undergraduate poet, Wright wrote poems with fierce patience and dedicated haste. The undergraduate magazine *Hika* published many; then, when Wright was a senior, John Crowe Ransom printed two poems in the *Kenyon Review*: "Lonely" and "Father." The latter poem is especially strong and tender, also curious: In its dreaminess, it resembles the poetry that Wright wrote fifteen or twenty years later—and not the narrative and reasonable iambic with which "Father" surrounded itself at the time; so often, in a poet's life, today's anomaly foreshadows tomorrow's invention.

A month after graduation Jim married his high school sweetheart Liberty Kardules, who had become a nurse, and taught for a few months at a school in Texas. The next year they spent in Austria, Wright with a Fulbright to study at the University of Vienna; he worked on the poems of Georg Trakl and the stories of Theodore Storm—both of whom he translated, both of whom contributed to his mature work. In the same year, Liberty gave birth to their first child, Franz.

Jim and I became acquainted in the autumn of 1954 and we were friends until he died. Although our friendship was crucial to us, each of us had closer friends among our generation. There were times when we became irritated with each other, and on the whole we had bad luck in getting together; mostly we connected by letter. Like any friendship among artists, ours was based on rivalry. I became aware of "James Wright" as early as 1952. When I was a senior at college an undergraduate literary magazine called *Coraddi* (from the Women's College of North Carolina; now the University of North Carolina at Greensboro) solicited work for an issue devoted to undergraduate writing everywhere. They printed a poem I sent them, and a year later mailed me the 1952 issue, which included James Wright from Kenyon College, with a poem called "Oenone to Paris . . .". It was a sonnet, pretty nifty, referring to:

> Some buttons made of artificial gold,
> These ordinary pumps, and rarely sheer
> Stockings to celebrate the turning year.
> I need an aspirin. My eyes are old.

Soon I began to see other Wright poems in visible places. I looked at work in magazines with an acquisitive eye, because I had become poetry editor for the upstarting *Paris Review*, which wanted to be the magazine of a generation. One day in the autumn of 1954, I solicited poetry from James Wright. Jim's answering letter (with poems) came from Seattle, 2 December 1954. ("Dear Mr. Hall, / Thank you very much for your extremely kind letter.") I knew of the University of Washington because Theodore Roethke taught there. By this time in the history of the American academy, poets had begun to make their livings as teachers—but they did not yet spend their lives teaching only Linebreaks 101. When Roethke taught his famous class in writing, he brought old poetry into it—whereby he filled the cistern as much as he emptied it. Deciding to support himself as a teacher, Jim pursued a conventional Ph.D. in English and wrote a thesis about Charles Dickens. In his academic career, by preference, Jim taught literature rather than Creative Writing.

The older poet resembled the younger. Roethke came from a background more prosperous than Wright's (Otto Roethke owned a greenhouse) but from the milltown of Saginaw in Michigan; Ann Arbor was Roethke's Kenyon. Both men were provincial, literary, and shy; both relied on comic routines to get them through social situations; both enjoyed sports, and when Jim took his Ph.D., Roethke's graduation present was a ticket to the world heavyweight championship bout of 1957 between Floyd Patterson and Pete Rademacher in Seattle; Jim and Ted attended the bout together. (Jim described that fight for me round-by-round.) And both men drank too much. Roethke was manic-depressive, delusional—suffering from a thought-disorder, not merely a mood-disorder—and several times hospitalized. If James was delusional, I do not know it, but like most poets he suffered from a bipolar mood disorder. Some alcoholics start from bipolarity; they drink to relieve depression (and become more depressed) or in mania drink to calm down (and induce depression). In the letters that we wrote each other—sometimes multi-page single-spaced letters like manic monologues—the bravado about drink was continuous.

More than drink, of course, our letters talked *poetry*. We talked about old poets—we both loved E. A. Robinson; not many did—and we talked of our friends and contemporaries. We worked over each other's things. Poets work together more than most people suppose, not institutionally in workshops but privately as friends and rivals. Most poets act as if they share a common endeavor. Competition between artists can be fierce but benign, dedicated to the art rather than to the artist, as when older athletes (sometimes) help younger ones who will succeed them. I remember a trivial gesture that may stand in for the serious generosity of many people. About the time my first book came out, Jim planned to submit *The Green Wall* to the Yale Younger Poets competition. I was visiting my parents' house outside New Haven. Jim wanted me to see the manuscript—and so I offered to deliver the book to the Yale University Press when I had read it. I handed his prizewinner to the receptionist.

Over the years, Jim's letters were full of Robert Bly, John Logan, Theodore Roethke, Galway Kinnell, Carolyn Kizer, Anne Sexton, Jean Valentine, Jane Cooper, Bill Merwin, Vassar Miller, Phil Levine, Dick Hugo, and . . . In our letters we talked prosody, enthralled by iambic; most of the old poetry we loved was metrical. We were so saturated with iambic that later we needed to jettison both meter and rhyme—most of our generation did—in favor of other tunes and musics. In *The Green Wall* Jim shows joyous skill in rhyme, linebreaks, and caesurae. His learning comes not from workshops but from love of Pope, Keats, Dunbar, Robinson, Hardy, Herrick, Marvell, and company. He takes pleasure in being champion of the socially unacceptable, as in "A Gesture by a Lady with an Assumed Name"—and, in the same words and without contradiction, he takes pleasure in rhyme and metrical inversion:

> Whether or not, how could she love so many,
> Then turn away to die as though for none?
> I saw the last offer a child a penny
> To creep outside and see the cops were gone.

Jim's medial inversion, third line, third foot, in those days would have us clapping our hands: "Get a load of *that!*"

His metrical style perfected itself in *Saint Judas*, for instance in the sonnet which supplies the title, which ends in a classic single line of resolution; only one ictus keeps it from the almost-rare fulfillment of the iambic paradigm: "I held the man for nothing in my arms." Three-quarters of us, if we had written the poem, would have wrecked the ending, diction and rhythm both, by a slack metaphor and an extra syllable: "I cradled the man for nothing in my arms." Jim's diction was as pure as his metric was resourceful and exact.

If *Saint Judas* was the best he could attain to, in the old mode, it was also the end of it. In 1958, in July, he wrote me a letter (I'm sure similar letters went to others) in which he announced that he was through writing poems. Another poet had mildly assaulted Jim in a review of the first *New Poets* anthology; Jim's first reaction had been thirty scurrilous epigrams and an insulting letter addressed to the reviewer . . . but now he turned his anger upon himself. In this letter he spoke of "denying the darker and wilder side of myself for the sake of subsisting on mere comfort—both academic and poetic." The first issue of Robert Bly's magazine *The Fifties*, which he read at this crucial point, arrived like a reproach. (He did not yet know Bly.) He told me: "So I quit. I have been betraying whatever was true and courageous . . . in myself and in everyone else for so long, that I am still fairly convinced that I have killed it. So I quit." In the letter he called himself "a literary operator (and one of the slickest, cleverest, most 'charming' concoctors of the do-it-yourself *New Yorker* verse among all current failures)."

A day later he wrote again, admitting that "I can't quit and go straight. I'm too deep in debt to the Olympian syndicate. They'd rub me out." (This was Roethke-talk, who during mania often alluded to The Mob.) Later he said, "It was my old, shriveling, iambic self that struck." He continued to write iambic, as he attacked his old iambic self; he was at the same time the fox and the hounds, turned upon himself in the corrosive iambics of "At the Executed Murderer's Grave," neatly berating himself for neatness—and of course beginning to find his way out. It was a way out, not really from iambic—arrangements of softer and louder syllables are guiltless—but from diction and thought he associated with iambic.

Jim visited Ann Arbor that August, an intense moment of

talk and merriment. In these years we met several times—at an MLA convention, where we both looked for work; at a poetry do at Wayne State in Detroit—and I discovered the pleasures of his companionship. He liked to laugh—a good storyteller, a fine mimic. With children he was especially inventive, playing little magic tricks; children could never get enough of him. For grown-ups he had another repertoire, mostly borrowed from comedians he admired. Like Roethke he did an exemplary W. C. Fields. He had yards of Jonathan Winters by heart. One brief bit I especially admired, and asked him to perform a thousand times. He stood assuming a humble, even pathetic posture— head tilted, arms akimbo—and crooned in his handsome voice, "By day, a humble butcher . . ." Then manic energy leapt into his face, he smiled broadly, his fingers clicked at this sides, and he gave a three-second impression of Bojangles, while his lit-up voice announced: "By night, a *fabulous tap-dancer!*" Thinking of him now, more than a decade after his death, I remember what Ezra Pound said about his friend Gaudier-Brzeska, killed in France in 1915: "He was the best fun in the world."

On his quick August visit, we planned that he would return with his family in the autumn, after the birth of their second child. They would come for the weekend when the University of Minnesota played Michigan in football. I would get tickets. They would drive—or Liberty would; Jim never learned to drive—for a long weekend of football and poetry. But the visit was a disaster. The drive to Ann Arbor seemed interminable, as Liberty parked at the side of the road when she needed to nurse the baby, a new son named Marshall. Then their car broke down;

they bought another used car and arrived late, exhausted, with Jim intensely nervous. He talked without stopping. He quoted page after page of prose and poetry, Dunbar's "Lament" at least twice. At one point, at a cocktail party we took them to, Jim recited German poetry for twenty minutes to an astonished assembly of mathematicians. Jim and I sat at the football game for perhaps four hours, getting there early to watch the warm-ups, but I'm not sure I spoke at all. Jim talked about free verse, iambic, wit, images, Dickens, Dickinson, Pope, James Stephens, football, Robert Bly, James Dickey, Ted Roethke, boxing, Liberty, Franz, Marshall, basketball . . . His voice was like the sea, when you stand at the rail of a ship watching the waves all day.

Maybe that night, maybe the next, Jim's good-natured, affable, unstoppable tirade suddenly turned black. Late at night he decided that *they* wanted him to go back to the mills. He made a speech about how he would never go back to the mills, no matter how much *they* tried to push him there; he had fought *them* all his life. And he stormed upstairs to bed. In the morning, he walked outside in the frost of early morning without eating or speaking. He leaned against an old oak tree and smoked Pall Malls for two hours, while Liberty ate breakfast, fed Franz and Marshall, packed, and loaded the car. Continually I slipped outside to try to talk with him; he mumbled and shook his head. He did not seem angry; he would not talk now, but he would write a letter. It was cold, and the white of his cigarette smoke mingled with the white of his breath. Feeling the cold, I would go back inside to warm up; then I would look out the window, see him there alone, and go back. When Liberty finished her chores they drove away.

A few days later, letters began arriving from Minneapolis. He remembered seeing me "forlorn and troubled in the wet leaves, both of you seeing us vanish." In one of these letters he told about saving his soldier's pay while he was in Japan. "I knew musicians and possible poets and even ordinary lovable human beings, and I saw them with brutal regularity going into Wheeling Steel, turning into stupid and resigned slobs with beer bellies and glassy eyes." Every now and then, he said, this madness flashed over him.

Although Jim had been drinking over the weekend, the problem did not begin with alcohol. When he returned to Minneapolis, the considerable torment of his life turned worse. He entered a mental hospital where he received electroshock for depression. In the new year, he and Liberty separated for the first time. They went back together, then parted again. Psychotherapy helped; it didn't cure. And—I suppose especially when separated from his family—the drinking turned worse. Once in a letter, April 23, 1959, he told me about attempting suicide (years earlier) by walking into the water near Seattle. His letters, like his poems, gave testimony to the day-to-day struggle of his life, which lasted—with restful respites, especially after his marriage to Annie—until he died, a struggle to live and make art, a struggle that the branch should not break.

Above the River, James Wright's "Complete Poems" of 1990, is testimony that it didn't. However beaten he was—some poems record defeat—James Wright was resilient. Even in the letters of 1959, the struggle to make poetry continued; it was identical to the struggle to live at all. Working away from iambic, which for a while seemed glib or complacent, he asked me for instructions in making syllabics, which had been my own first alternative metric. Other poets excited him. He wrote enthusiastically about John Logan, Robert Bly, and Geoffrey Hill, whom he had come greatly to admire. Then there were terrible setbacks: on September 3, 1960, a woeful letter: "I really am sick this time."

In July of 1961, my family and I spent a week at Robert and Carol Bly's Minnesota farmhouse, visiting at the same time as Louis and Dorothy Simpson with their two children. Jim was living alone, teaching summer school; he came out to join us for two weekends. From April on, his letters dwelt upon this possible getting-together, and in June he was writing agendas, numbered paragraphs of questions that we must take up with Robert when we were all together. He conspired with me against Robert because of Robert's perceived dogmatism about meter. (In his formal ambivalence, Jim was always sneaking off to write an iambic poem, showing it to me, and asking me not to tell Robert.) Out at the farm, Robert and Carol, Louis and Dorothy, and my wife and I lived an ebullient holiday, competing in badminton and swimming as well as in poetry and jokes. Jim came out from Minneapolis on the bus, a three- or four-hour ride. He was sad and lonesome, living a little to the side of the rest of us: because he was divorced, without his children, and drinking too much.

A few years earlier, Jim and I had added another facet to our relationship. I became a member of the poetry board for the Wesleyan University Press, which took Jim's *Saint Judas* for its beginning poetry series. When we accepted Jim's book, I became his editor, which meant that I gave him my opinions—as we had always done—and also passed him advice from the other editors. After *Saint Judas*, James submitted a collection of poems called *Amenities of Stone* that included old-style James Wright iambic poems as well as early surreal free verse. It was perhaps confused but it was powerful: Wesleyan's board was unanimous in accepting it. Then, just after the Minnesota gathering—on July 29, 1961, with the book already scheduled for publication—Jim withdrew *Amenities of Stone* from publication. If it had appeared, it would have shown Wright's transformation in process, almost in slow motion. Because he withdrew *Amenities*, James Wright's metamorphosis shocked his readers when *The Branch Will Not Break* came out in 1963. Many reviewers disparaged it; but the new style gathered its own constituency. "The cool master of iambic," said the critical caricature, "sheds his costume and walks naked." It is still difficult for many readers to love both sides of James Wright—Neruda and Robinson, Trakl and Hardy.

The critical caricature is distorted not only because it is a stick figure but because of an invalid image: Nakedness is always a new costume. The many sides of James Wright are not nearly so discontinuous as they first appear. If we ignore either the discontinuities or the continuities, we ignore matters large in his poems. For my taste, there are three high moments in Wright's work. First came the height of traditional sound and structure, already handsome in *The Green Wall*, achieving its zenith in the poems of *Saint Judas*—including "At the Executed Murderer's Grave," which derides its own tradition and achievement. The second height was *The Branch Will Not Break*, a putative opposite, where simple images embody almost unbearable tension between deathward suffering and the desire to endure, to love, and to enjoy the world's pleasures. At best, the opposites come together, as in a famous enjambment: "I would break / into blossom." Sometimes the insistence on blossoming is contradicted (or even mocked) by a clear evidence of breakage. Always the battle (conflict makes energy) takes place before us in these poems—as it takes place within us.

The third height, and best poetry of all, turns up in the last two books, but before he could reach this final eminence his work went through a lesser moment. Fine poems in *Shall We Gather at the River* mingle with slackness, which increases in the new poems of *Collected Poems* and in *Two Citizens*. This essay is no place for dwelling on failures—all poets fail—but let me suggest that in his slack patches, Wright abandons oxymoronic images, often to rely on a storyteller's voice which rambles, and, proclaiming certainty, seems uncertain. Sometimes when he fails he insists not on beauty (which is conflicted) but on prettiness (which isn't) against his own ugly experience.

At his best, from *The Green Wall* through the posthumous *This Journey*, Wright gathers true feeling—often feeling for the oppressed (internal and external)—into lines of great sensuous beauty; at his best, he had the finest ear of his generation. In *To a Blossoming Pear Tree* and *This Journey*, the stance of the storyteller or performer (awkward in *Two Citizens*) energizes the page in prose poems like "The Wheeling Gospel Tabernacle." Better still, in a poem like "The Best Days," or even more "The

Last Days," everything comes together—vision and vowel, capacity for suffering and capacity for joy, even Ohio and Italy. Each of these poems begins with the epigraph from Virgil, *optima dies prima fugit*, and by the end of "The Last Days," when the poet rescues a bee drowning in the sweet juice of a pear, James Wright has found his Ohio in Virgil's Mantua:

> The best days are the first
> To flee, sang the lovely
> Musician born in this town
> So like my own.
> I let the bee go
> Among the gasworks at the edge of Mantua.

Of course Jim's Italy is not merely the peninsula but also a literary tradition: Italy of Catullus, Virgil, Ovid; Italy of frosty Protestants looking for sun, northerners who come south and like the bee in the pear almost die in the ecstasy of southern flesh. The Germans made their sensuous pilgrimage, notably Jim's beloved Goethe with his *Italian Journey*: and there were the great poets of our language: Keats, Shelley, Landor, Browning, Ezra Pound; American novelists discovered an Italy also: Henry James, Edith Wharton, and even William Dean Howells—the *other* literary figure born in Martins Ferry, Ohio.

In haste to arrive at Italy, I have bypassed some miseries. In 1963, the year he published *The Branch Will Not Break*, James Wright was fired by the University of Minnesota. Among the professors voting to deny him tenure was his friend the poet Allen Tate, which was hurtful. Jim missed classes because he got drunk; Jim got into barroom fistfights and spent time in the drunktank. It may be noted that Professor Berryman of the University of Minnesota, not renowned for sobriety, taught not in the Department of English but in the Department of Humanities.

Jim taught two years at Macalester College in St. Paul, then won a Guggenheim. In 1966, he took a good job at Hunter College in New York where he remained until his death. Soon after he moved to New York he met Edith Ann Runk—Annie—and they were married in the Riverside Church in April of 1967. Although one cannot say that they lived happily ever after—Jim returned to the hospital with breakdowns—his fortunes in large part reversed themselves. Annie was tender, affectionate, and supportive of his poetry. Jim's work gained recognition, which can be tracked through prizes: In 1971 Brandeis gave him its prize in poetry; that year his *Collected Poems* appeared, for which he received the Pulitzer Prize; then the Academy of American Poets awarded him its ten-thousand-dollar fellowship. Increasingly, he and Annie spent summers in Italy or France; sometimes Jim took a term away from teaching and they would travel among hotels in Europe—quietly, soberly, enjoying pleasures of laziness, love, and work.

The year before he died was a good one, maybe more crowded with writing than any other time in his life. January through September, 1979, Jim and Annie traveled in Europe; he rose at four to work on his new poems. He wrote letters frequently, full of plans and vigor. Then, there was a sore throat.

Diagnosis was difficult. It was late in the autumn back in New York before his cancer was discovered, a little rough spot behind his tongue. At first it seemed curable: Oncology would shrink the tumor by x-ray and surgery would cut it out; Jim was worried that the operation would curtail his speaking of poems. But the tumor would not shrink and there was no operation. Annie wrote old friends who alerted each other by telephone. Jim's last outing was an appearance at President Carter's poetry party at the White House in January of 1980. Then he entered Mt. Sinai. Annie arranged visits from old friends of his generation. Galway Kinnell was teaching in Hawaii then, but found a reading in New York that allowed him to visit. Also came Philip Levine, Mark Strand, Robert Bly, Louis Simpson . . . Jim reconciled two old friends who had quarreled. Because Jim looked bad—teeth out, hair patchy, thin—and because he was an old-fashioned male, he could not bear his women friends to see him. Jane Cooper and Jean Valentine prevailed, but only for a moment.

When I visited him the first time, on Saturday the first of March, it was NCAA basketball tournament time. When I saw Jim a year before, we had talked excitedly about the confrontation of Michigan State and Indiana State, Magic Johnson and Larry Bird. Jim and I had always talked sports. Thus I arrived at Mt. Sinai—to see my wretched racked friend—booming out noise about an approaching basketball tournament with a heartiness that tried to disguise fear and panic. Jim was polite but he was not in the mood to talk about sports. I quieted down; the subjects we spoke of were poetry, friendship, and mortality.

It was a room for four—noisy, shabby, and dirty. Behind him on the wall were tacked dozens of photographs, mostly of his friends' children. Jim couldn't talk—the tracheotomy—but he scrawled questions and answers on a yellow pad. The terrible thing was his coughing, as his throat tried to expel the machinery of its breathing-hole: Foam erupted, tinged with pink. Annie asked him if I could look at his new poems; he was still tinkering. So I first read *This Journey* as I sat beside Jim's bed in Mt. Sinai, scarcely able to distinguish one word from another; I let my eyes scan across lines, down pages, and I murmured, "Wonderful, Jim, wonderful."

Three and a half weeks later Annie called me, the afternoon of March 25th, to say that Jim had died that morning. The funeral at the Riverside Church—in the Little Chapel where they had been married—was crowded with poets lamenting. The friends from California and Hawaii, who had visited Jim alive, did not fly in again for the memorial service, but Robert Bly was there, Louis Simpson, Gibbons Ruark, David Ignatow, Jane Cooper, Mark Strand, Tom Lux, C. K. Williams, Jean Valentine, John Haines, T. Weiss, Harvey Shapiro . . . The organ played "Shall We Gather at the River" but we did not sing it. The eulogy did not avoid the harshness of Jim's life.

As it happened, I had seen him one more time—three days before he died, three weeks after my first visit. He had been moved to a hospice in the Bronx called Calvary. It was a relief to see him there after the squalor of Mt. Sinai. His single room was quiet, clean, tidy. As I walked in the corridors while nurses attended to Jim, I saw a skeletal young girl with no hair, the skin tight on her skull; I saw a young man with a leg amputated, bandages over arms and head—*yet* tenderness and reverence were palpable in Calvary's air. In the corridor a young black woman sang softly to herself and with her arms clasped together danced a few steps. Jim's nurses and helpers touched him and called him pet names.

Annie was there with her niece Karen East; Jim was fond of Karen. I stayed for a couple of hours, mostly without speaking. At one point Jim started to write me a note, and paused after the third word. On his yellow scratch pad I watched him write, "Don, I'm dying"—and then, after a tiny pause, as short as a linebreak—"to eat ice-cream from a tray." Jim stared continually at Annie as if he memorized her to take her with him. Once he stared fiercely at her back while she looked out the window at wet snow falling late in March in the dingy Bronx. He signaled to me that he wanted Annie. I relayed the message and she stood above him while he gazed and his jaw shifted from side to side. He held her hands, then took them to his lips and kissed them.

When Annie left the room briefly he was agitated. Although he was virtually speechless, he rasped one sentence: "Don, this is it." I nodded. When Annie returned he took up the manuscript of *This Journey*, which he had asked Annie to photocopy for mailing to several friends, who would work with her to make the final book. Because I was there, he could hand it to me, and he improvised a small ritual. He wrote on the manila envelope, among other words, "I can do no more." Ceremonially he asked Annie and Karen to sign as witnesses. He added the date and handed his last poems over.

LONG LIVE THE DEAD

Frequently, a writer must read for the sake of work: checking facts, absorbing background. (Sometimes I accept a commission because of the reading required; one should never review a book one doesn't already want to read.) Really, disinterested reading—reading by whim or chance, without conscious purpose—contributes most to a writer's interest. Grazing idly in a literary pasture, we discover manners of language alien to our habits, which allow us new invention. If we stick to what we already know, we stick to what we already do.

Maybe a dozen years ago, I picked up Edward Gibbon's *Decline and Fall of the Roman Empire*. When I was an undergraduate looking into the history of English prose style, I learned the noises Gibbon made—great larruping controlled periods, syntactic probes or explorations—but I never took him in. When I was ready for him, a dozen years ago, I took him in *whole*, headlong, in an ecstasy of disinterested reading. I read nothing for months except Gibbon, poleaxed by rhythms, by syntax that branched like a maple, by irony administered through sentence structure.

Gibbon would tell me that the emperor requested *or* required; the emperor required *or rather* requested; the emperor requested *or perhaps* required . . . Will you make up your mind, Mr. Gibbon? No, Mr. Gibbon will not make up his mind (unless he *knows*) but he will tilt one way or another; by his grammar, diction, and word order, he will let me understand the bent of his mind as well as his mind's doubts of its own bent. Later when I read Tacitus—I hastened to devour the newly discovered literature of history—I would find that Gibbon's *or* descended directly from Tacitus's judicious *aut*. Gibbon made his monument from the relics and ruins he wandered among: Reading his sources, like Procopius, I watched how he borrowed here and rejected there to build his own edifice—a temple of our language, a world-book encompassing not only its ostensible subject but the life's wisdom of an extraordinary mind: like Chaucer's *Canterbury Tales*, like Shakespeare's plays, like Dickens.

Reading Gibbon I discovered the pleasure of reading two books at once. While I studied the decline and fall of Rome, I also attended to the mind of the later eighteenth century. (The first volumes of *Decline* appeared, appropriately enough, in the same year as Jefferson's "Declaration.") Reading him, I developed a sense for what was 76 A.D. and what was 1776. Double-reading can happen whenever writing is historical; Hawthorne's *Scarlet Letter* is 1848 more than it is seventeenth-century Salem. This phenomenon abounds in translation. Dryden's *Aeneid*, the best translation in our language, gives us first century B.C. imperial Rome (if not the mythic age Vergil conjures) but reveals as well the mind and spirit of England late in the seventeenth century.

To discern this doubleness, I grant you, you need to know something of Vergil and something of Dryden's time. The more extended our disinterested reading, the more complex and rewarding each occasion becomes.

Gibbon led me back to the Greeks, to the narrative of Xenophon, to the myth of Herodotus, and to the vast skeptical humanity of Thucydides, greatest of all historians. Tacitus is the best of the Romans, ironic and fierce and adult, while Livy makes stories for Roman schoolboys or English ones—patriotic tales for Augustan Youth. Running out of classic historians, I found Hume's *History of England*—nobly made, only outdone by Gibbon—as well as Macaulay's, whose gorgeous prose expends itself in sentimental pursuit. Macaulay is as biased as the American Motley, whose history of the Dutch Republic praises Protestant Burgher Good at the expense of Spanish Catholic Bad. I spoke earlier about the glories of American historians, when I praised Henry Adams as historian.

Bias is common in a narrative history—the kind I read—where the writer busies himself devil-and-angeling: See Macaulay on the Irish or William Penn; see Harvard's John Fisk, whose naive social Darwinism diminishes the utility and beauty of his American narrative. Shelby Foote intends to be evenhanded about the Civil War—and writes beautiful narrative history—but in late chapters we discern dimly the strains of "Dixie." Even Gibbon is complacent in his Enlightenment attitude toward religion and superstition: At one point he reassures the reader that an emperor was intelligent, *although* he believed that planets controlled human destiny. Until quite recently, Gibbon tells us, fairly bright people believed such glop.

If the dead historians were conspicuously unfair—to women, Indians, Jews, conquered peoples, Catholics, barbarians, Protestants, Arabs, Africans, Asians, Buddhists, and Muslims— our contemporary literary culture is universally unfair to the dead. I suggest a reform platform: a New Deal for the Dead. Reading history has everything to do with this platform, because such reading shuts down the provinces of one's complacency. There were cultures in the Dark Ages that eschewed capital punishment, medieval societies that would look upon us as barbaric in our judicial murders. Neither can we consider ourselves uniquely violent: Reading history shows that Hitler and Stalin were normative leaders.

History is the story of wicked power, employed in the selfish services of the powerful, normally exercised with convictions of benignity.

When we rail at the dead for their hate speech, we announce our moral superiority to human history. Reading contemporary reviews of somebody's nineteenth-century collected letters, we discover that our reviewers belong to the first moral generation born upon this planet. The unborn will never forgive us our conceit. What will our other major vices be? Violence private and public? Affluence and starvation, gluttony and deprivation? Our conceit will appear quaint and despicable.

Reading history has touched or transformed my poetry, giving me images or anecdotes that find common humanity among disparate eras and cultures. As well, Gibbon especially drew my attention to neglected possibilities of language, especially long controlled sentences in which syntax (enforcing its own drumbeat or rhythmic dance) provides or enables judgment. And Gibbon encouraged me to depart from the imitation of common speech (cf. William Carlos Williams or Robert Creeley), a practice which has made wonderful poems but which seems worn out for the moment. Gibbon's Latinate starchiness allows or demands exact expression, no flurry of approximation but one precise if sometimes obscure word. Is the lying-down body prone or supine? The tone of a vocabulary establishes a vocabulary of tones—and revives the old humor (extant as late as W. C. Fields, "Major Hoople," and Marianne Moore) where the joke is the distance between elevated vocabulary and ordinary or debased action: "Indicate the way to my abode. / I'm fatigued and I desire to retire."

Are such jokes elitist because they demand vocabulary? We live in a country and a time of many tribes and many vocabularies, in a culture that tends toward the centrifugal. If each tribe desires autonomy, each wants its solitude contradicted by the gregariousness of praise and reward. When tribes define themselves by tongue, universal recognition requires multilingualism—but, alas, if we are multicultural, we are also monolingual. How stupid that—when they dip into Spanish—I no longer understand the poems of Martín Espada and Jimmy Santiago Baca.

Multicultural exchange or appreciation requires learning both linguistic and cultural, even when this exchange remains horizontal. For a profounder extension of humanity, we need vertical multiculturalism as well as horizontal—in which historical reading (of literature, of archaeology, of history) acquaints us with Egypt and China, Sumeria and the Hanseatic League. Reading *Gilgamesh* is an antidote to a provinciality both geographic and temporal. Long live the dead.

READING, SORROW, AND DREAD

My life's project began in the second grade when I was seven and whooping cough kept me home from school. I grew bored with radio soap operas, fifteen minutes long, telling stories about Ma Perkins or Mary Noble Backstage Wife. I had brought my storybook home from school; in my boredom I read it over and over. Thus I became fluent at reading for the first time, and discovered the bliss of abandonment to print, to word and story. From the love of reading eventually derived the desire to write, a lifelong commitment to making things that might (if I were diligent, talented, and lucky) resemble the books I loved reading.

Reading and writing have filled the days of my life, good times and bad ones, reflecting passages of love, despair, anger, and joy. Reading and writing take their places even in mourning or in fear of death. By words I remember my first consciousness of mortality. When I was nine and a great-aunt died, I lay in bed after the funeral, staying awake to repeat a sentence in my head: "Now death has become a reality." It was as if I were reading my biography, and "at the age of nine," the book said, "death became a reality for Donald Hall." A couple of years later, I read over and over again a novel called *Jimmy Sharswood* by Roy Helton, a North Carolina poet (I found out later) whom Robert Frost admired. The eponymous boy-hero died, and I reread the book in order to weep, not to escape from mortality but to embrace it—or rather to embrace the idea of it; maybe one pursues literary death in order to evade the real thing. Samuel Taylor Coleridge noted a fear that afflicts the scrupulous literary mind: "Poetry—excites us to artificial feelings—callous to real ones."

However dubious or healthy the reason, when I find someone's death insupportable, poetry is useful. I find solace in entering someone else's grief, intense as the moment's shudder, across centuries or even across languages and cultures. A poem I first look for is Henry King's "The Exequy." John Donne's executor, King lived from 1592 to 1669; in 1617 he married Ann Berkely when she was seventeen; she died at twenty-four and King addressed her in tetrameter couplets:

> Never shall I
> Be so much blessed as to descry
> A glimpse of thee, till that day come
> Which shall the earth to cinders doom,
> And a fierce fever must calcine
> The body of this world like thine,
> (My little world!)

His grief over the young woman dead of a fever is more painful than this morning's obituary page; always my loss takes dour satisfaction in Henry King's company.

Much poetry makes itself out of dysphoria, an energetic conflict: Pleasure of language assaults as it embodies the statement of misery. Even the oldest poetry: Reading a translation from the Sumerian, we hear the lament of Gilgamesh, wretched over the death of his blood-brother Enkidu. These words come from the Penguin prose translation by N. K. Sanders:

> Gilgamesh began to rage like a lion, like a lioness robbed of her whelps. This way and that he paced round the bed, he tore out his hair and strewed it around.
>
> . . . seven days and seven nights he wept for Enkidu, until the worm fastened on him. Only then he gave him up to the earth . . .

Three thousand years later, we all know the same wild or petulant grief.

And what do we next endure or feel? When we grieve for another we always grieve for ourselves. Gilgamesh says: "What my brother is now, that shall I be when I am dead." Even for Henry King, although his Christianity is confident of survival, his bride's death leads to thoughts of his own.

> Thou wilt not wake
> Till I thy fate shall overtake;
> Till age or grief, or sickness must
> Marry my body to the dust
> It so much loves; and fill the room
> My heart keeps empty in thy tomb.
> Stay for me then; I will not fail
> To meet thee in that hallow vale.

It is a matter of course, in the lives we endure, that each of us must one day acknowledge forthcoming death—unless we drop dead of an unpredicted heart attack or a random bullet. One day we will hear the oncologist say, "I'm afraid the prognosis is discouraging." Some years ago a young doctor with thick glasses cleared his throat before he told me, "You have colon cancer." After the operation my chances of making five years were two out of three, but two years later the carcinoma metastasized to my liver. With two thirds of that organ removed, together with all discernible disease, my chances dwindled to one in three. From day to day I feel healthy and energetic; I am happy in work and love; it is a good patch of my life—but every quarter I do bloodwork, and I am aware that one day the results may bear bad tidings.

It is not grief that one feels for oneself but dread of the grief of others. I do not speak of altruism. Doubtless I fear the pain of dying, but when I expect my own death, mostly I feel not fear or dread but wretchedness that my daily routine must conclude: no more glancing through the *Globe* early in the morning while drinking black coffee; no more bodily love; no more working at the desk all day—the long engagement with language, which I adore as a sculptor loves wood or clay, as a musician melody and tempo; no more sleepy visions of the Red Sox losing another game as I go to bed.

And no more reading. Approaching death touches on reading as on everything else. For one thing, reading will not distract us from dread. Oh, if we merely foresee the moment of ether and the knife, certain books may occupy us. Before my first large operation, gallbladder in 1969, I read *Portnoy's Complaint*. I laughed, page by page, until the orderlies rolled me to the operating room. But then I couldn't finish the book for a month: When an incision is healing, we avoid books that make us laugh.

With my more recent diseases and operations, surgery has

been my least concern. When they make the incision, what will they *find*? What will the laboratory's dyes and microscopes discover, peering at cell structure? Not even Philip Roth distracts from such concerns; not even spy sagas. For that matter, I cannot read junk for diversion. Finer sensibilities than my own have relaxed with Agatha Christie and Zane Grey—but under conditions of pain and distress, slack language causes me pain and distress. What can we read, in mortal circumstances? I cannot concentrate enough to read Linda Gregg's poems or Flaubert's letters to George Sand or Nicholas Grimal's new history of old Egypt; the words of others quickly metamorphose into my own anxieties, and I read two pages without reading a sentence. John's Gospel I can take a few verses at a time; his doctrines of love raise me up—but then his concentration on last things cuts to the bone.

Depressed over my probable brevity, I find my reading mocked by my own acquisitiveness. Part of my pleasure in reading has always been pride in accumulation. I read to use what I read, for understanding and for writing; take away that future use, and my reading mocks me: If I am not to live more than a wretched year or two—I think at a low point—what am I reading *for*? When I should be able to read for the joy of a book's beauty, I cannot. For the first time in my life, reading depresses me; the old comforts fall away; I might as well feel miserable watching Vanna White spin a wheel.

For weeks after my last operation—frail and without energy, sleeping ten hours—I looked in my house at all the books I had not read, and wept for my inability to read them. Or I looked at great books I had read too quickly in my avidity—telling myself that I would return to them later. There is never a *later* but for most of my life I have believed in *later*.

Wherever I turned to escape depression, the place I turned to became the place I had left. When I found comfort in love, love turned bitter with the notion of abandoning it. King Gilgamesh, realizing that what had happened to Enkidu would happen to him, journeyed to the end of the earth—with suffering, overcoming terrible obstacles—to seek counsel of the one man who had avoided dying, a Babylonian Noah called Utnapishtim. But Utnapishtim could not pass immortality on.

Like reading, writing has always provided a dream of acquisition: so many poems, so many books. After my last operation I had a book to finish, half-drafted when I learned about my liver. There were children's books begun, with grandchildren on my mind. There were poems to work over, if I had time. A new poem, out of my illness, nibbled at the edges of consciousness.

Three and a half weeks after my lobectomy, I returned to *Life Work*; then I started the new poem; then I took up old poems again—changing a word, altering a linebreak or a mark of punctuation. At first I worked only in brief intent bursts, ten or twenty minutes, trying to tidy things up. Working again I forgot the statistics of survival—for minutes on end; then for hours. Able to write, I was able to read again—to return to Adam Smith's *Wealth of Nations*, which I had interrupted; to read Charles Simic's new poems; to reread Chekhov's stories about the lives and deaths, miserable and exalted, of every man and every woman.

HENRY MOORE'S DAY

Every day, Henry Moore woke at 7:30, made a pot of tea downstairs in the kitchen, and took it back to the bedroom, where he and his wife Irina drank two cups apiece. At 8:00 they listened to the BBC news and weather. On December 20, 1963, Moore heard that the day would be fine, and he was pleased; bad weather had been keeping him from working outside on his big, new Locking Piece. He descended to eat breakfast and made more tea at 8:30. Some days, if it's 8:34 and Moore had not yet emerged from the bathroom, Irina would call up the stairs, threatening him in her delicate Russian accent, "Henery, shall I make the tea?" Yorkshiremen think that only Yorkshiremen know how to make tea.

At breakfast he opened the morning's mail. Moore's feelings about the mail were ambivalent. He looked forward to it, and if there weren't a quantity he was disappointed, yet answering mail was a great tedium. By 1963, when he turned sixty-five, Moore was rich and famous; either condition makes for correspondence. Whole drawers concealed unanswered letters. Now and then he took a day away from work and dictated to Mrs. Tinsley; a week later he felt just as far behind. This particular morning (when I spent the day with him) there was a letter from *Harper's Magazine* asking him to write an article on Giacometti; a medical charity asked him to donate a sculpture; the Oxford University Press wanted him to do an illustration for a book; three dealers wrote for information about Henry Moores they had for sale; his tax accountant asked a passing question; an American Ph.D. candidate inquired about "the influence of vorticism on your work." Unlike many eminent folk, Moore found it unsettling to leave letters unanswered. He would deny a publisher's request to do a book of lithographs, but deny it at great length, giving many reasons.

The Moores ate breakfast in the long dining room at the front of the house, a pleasant room full of paintings and flowers. Henry dated the envelopes and passed to Irina the letters in which she might be interested. At 9:00 his sculptural assistants arrived and started to work in the new studios in the field behind the house. By 9:30 the mail was read and Moore usually began his day's work, often in one of the small old studios in front of Hoglands—which was the name of the Moores' whitewashed, asymmetrical, fifteenth-century farm cottage. They moved in 1940 from London, an hour or so away, to this house in the hamlet of Perry Green, near the village of Much Hadham, in the county of Hertfordshire. To the right of Hoglands a series of sheds and outbuildings trailed away toward the road. There was a garage for the Rover, and an open-ended shed housing a ping-pong table. Moore played a rough game of ping-pong. He crouched at his end of the table with his eyes gleaming, shifting on the balls of his feet, and lashed out an eccentric service. His backhand was good when he was set for it, but he had trouble moving the paddle over quickly enough. Sometimes instead of trying he struck at the ball with his left hand, and occasionally his bare palm hit an ace. "That *counts*, doesn't it?"

Beyond the ping-pong shed were three old studios, his only studios until he bought more land behind the house in 1956. By 1963 he used the first—a long, low, dark room—mostly for patinating bronzes. Moore didn't paint his sculptures as some artists do, but chose his stones with an eye to color, and stained his bronzes a wide range of tints by swabbing them with chemicals and buffing them. His small middle studio was mostly a storeroom, full of tiny plaster maquettes and pieces of bone or flint. His third studio, which Moore called "the far room," was his sanctum. He could reach it only by stepping outside the storeroom, into some shrubbery, and then up through a doorway. From the road or from Hoglands, it was a doorless room, a secret place like the imagination of the artist.

Moore seldom planned his work schedule in advance: "I let the morning decide." The sunny December morning decided that he would work on the Locking Piece, but he would wait until the sun was higher. He would start by finishing the waxes of small sculptures in the far room. Moore's small bronzes were cast by the lost-wax method, generally in an edition of ten. He finished each wax himself, correcting minor deviations from his original plaster and sometimes adding marks which wax will take and plaster won't; therefore each of his small pieces was at least a little different from its siblings.

That December morning, he arrived in the chilly workroom just before 9:30, wearing a long blue-and-white-striped butcher's apron. He lit a kerosene burner, and turned on a small two-bar electric heater. By ten o'clock the temperature had risen to 50 degrees. Meager winter sun entered through the transparent roof, and Moore used a gooseneck lamp to throw a special light on the waxes. He sat in a wicker chair, the wax in front of him mounted on a little turntable so that he could reach all sides easily.

His secret room was cluttered with a thousand objects, most of which had put in time on his turntable. There were plaster maquettes from twenty-five years back, including tiny versions of the stringed figures of the late thirties—white bowls and baskets strung like harps. There were photographs of big sculptures on the walls, and there were shelves and shelves of bones, flints, pebbles—natural objects which were sources of his forms—and small sculptures resembling bones, flints, and pebbles. When Moore wanted to modify or add to a bone shape, he made a plaster cast of the bone and then built onto it. The room was a mint of forms, a magic closet. It was here that the new shapes—even a bronze thirty feet wide and sixteen feet high for the North Plaza of Lincoln Center—were born from a piece of flint and a pair of modeling hands.

In front of Moore that morning was the wax of a new helmet head in two parts; the wax was a deep red, and the helmet resembled a red plastic toy for a Martian child. One part was the exterior shell, a sort of knight's helmet swelling out a little at top and bottom. The solid back resembled a woman's torso, like so many of Moore's shapes. Into the hollow front fitted the second part of the sculpture, a slim standing trunk that branched into eyes at the top. Moore was adjusting the angle at which the internal piece stood, adding bits of wax to the base. He rolled strips of wax between his fingers to make them pliable, warmed a spatula in the flame of an alcohol lamp, then smoothed flat the added wax. Sometimes he could not find his tool, and glanced distraught over the jumble of surfaces around him, and blamed his assistants the way one blames a child for anything out of place.

The alcohol lamp flickered and went out. He stood up and stretched (working over these waxes is a sleepy, relaxing thing to do; he must pay attention, but this is not *inventing*) and refilled his lamp in the storeroom next door. When he returned he ignited a strip of newspaper at the electric fire to light the lamp again. After ten minutes more of delicate smoothing, the helmet head was ready to go back to the founder and become bronze.

Then he began work on the wax of an upright figure, a totem-poleish piece that needed adjustments to most of its facets. At ten minutes past ten there was a knock on the studio door. Mrs. Tinsley was sorry to disturb him but Mr. Jackson had come with the photographs. Mr. Jackson entered with a stack of eight-by-ten prints. They were pictures of Moore at work in this room. Moore approved, and Mr. Jackson, who had waited for a sunny day to drive out from Hampstead, left to photograph more sculptures in back of Hoglands.

Half an hour later Moore finished the upright figure and decided it was time for elevenses. Apron off, he walked back to the house and talked with Mary, his seventeen-year-old daughter home from school for the holidays, about the dance he was driving her to that night. Mrs. Tinsley had a telegram for him, and Irina was afraid there would not be enough milk for the coffee. Since the day was fine they sat on the sun porch at the southern side of the house, across the hall from the dark dining room. Moore sat among Irina, Mary, Mrs. Tinsley, Sheila the cook, and Mrs. Barber the part-time cleaning woman. Then the phone rang for Henry—a friend had just returned from Los Angeles and wanted to tell Henry about the Moore show there—and when he returned his coffee was cold.

By 11:15 the cookies were eaten, the coffee was finished, and everyone was back at work. It was time for Moore to visit the big new studios at the bottom of the garden, where two assistants had been working since nine o'clock. He walked through the hall, past the stairs and the office, between the old and the new living rooms. The end of the hall was a small gallery of sculpture and ceramics, mostly pre-Columbian and medieval English. Then he entered a glassed-in vestibule with doors on either side. To the right was the front of the house and the old studios; to the left was the garden and the new studios. The floor was thick with mats for foot-scraping, and under a bench stood Wellingtons in a row—Wellingtons are high rubber boots worn over socks—for visitors who took a muddy walk over the acreage behind Hoglands.

Henry Moore put on a sporty blue-checked coat, a soft checked hat turned down all around, and blue mittens; then he walked out the left door toward the new studios. Just past the vestibule was a greenhouse where Irina kept her sophisticated collection of cacti. Farther on, fruit trees which Irina had espaliered marked the end of the old garden, after which the level lowered a few steps and the new garden began. Informal borders of shrubs, annuals, and perennials curved among hedges and trees, and here Irina Moore passed many waking hours. A hired gardener did the heavy work, but the garden was Irina's passion and creation. Her borders fitted the landscape and its season; in autumn the garden blazed with chrysanthemums and dahlias. But her work extended past borders: In a corner of land five hundred yards from the house, Irina had planted bluebells where her husband left old plasters of large sculptures to break into unpredictable shapes. Every spring, fragmented white Henry Moores hovered like ghosts above masses of blue flowers.

Moore used the new land partly as a private sculpture park. He kept one copy of most of his bronzes, and because these sculptures traveled to exhibitions and came back again he walked past a rotating show of his work every time he visited the new studios. Today he passed his King and Queen, that archaic pair of rulers, perched on top of a small hillock. A little farther was a Glenkiln Cross, half-cross half-torso struggling toward definition. Elsewhere were a seated draped figure and a warrior perpetually falling to the ground. As Moore passed them he noticed different things: Maybe one of them had gone dead for him, and he wondered why; maybe another looked better in one kind of light, or from a particular angle. His old work provided Moore lessons in making sculpture.

At the end of the new land were the gardener's cottage, a cutting garden, a greenhouse full of potted begonias, fuchsias and datura lilies, and a vegetable garden. Nearby were the two new studios, brick with big doors so that large plasters mounted on wheeled platforms could be pushed outside. A miscellany of large bronzes stood on platforms outside the studios, and inside were more sculptures in various stages—from big bronzes awaiting patination to armatures, the skeletal interiors of to-morrow's large plasters.

Hoglands was Moore's sculpture factory, complete with assistants as factory workers. Traditionally, the master sculptor has workers to help him, either young apprentice sculptors like Moore's assistants or craftsmen: professional stone carvers, wood carvers, or metal workers. Rodin had thirty assistants at one time—as Moore was quick to point out—and many of the best sculptors have served terms as assistants to an elder. Moore never did, and never sought help until he was almost forty, but now he cherished assistance as a device allowing him to produce more work. Today his assistants were Isaac Witkin and Ron Swan, with Witkin as foreman. A burly, round-faced South African, he had established a reputation of his own in London. Though some assistants felt unhappy in their work—it was just a job; you never saw enough of Moore, who was always on the telephone, or sitting on a committee in London, or showing visitors around the studios—others like Witkin were enthusiastic. He didn't want to be influenced by Moore's forms but by his spirit. (Moore was conscious of the danger of influence, and never looked at his assistants' own sculpture unless he was asked; if they knew he wouldn't be looking, they wouldn't be tempted to try to please him.) "Something of the man himself rubs off," Witkin said—and you realized "how green you are in form knowledge."

Of the five sculptures that Witkin had worked over in his two years as an assistant, the Locking Piece was his favorite. "I've never seen Henry so *involved* as with this one." The Locking Piece, in its final shape, is a generally circular bronze, nine feet high, in two parts that fit together like a child's puzzle. It doesn't resemble any one thing—it's not like the King and Queen, or one of Moore's family groups, which express the image of their title—but it is full of different images as you walk around it, as you focus on one facet or another. A portion of it looks like an elephant's foot; there are scraps of landscape and of natural objects; there are bits and pieces of many faces, including a fragment that resembles T. S. Eliot's nose. The more abstract a sculpture is, the more inclusive it can be of form experience. Walking around the completed Locking Piece, the observer encounters a series of soft explosions of recollection; forms become other forms: A hill from one angle is a torso from another, accomplishing a sort of wit in the shift of scale. The Locking Piece is the end result of thousands of things seen and things touched.

Moore had some clear ideas about its sources. It began, like most of Moore's work, from observation of nature. In digging the garden on their newly acquired land, the Moores uncovered a graveyard of animal bones, an old butcher's depository. Much sculpture climbed out of that grave. One day, puttering among the bones, Moore noticed the way a joint fitted and worked. A short time later, as he was sitting idly, perhaps in conversation, his hands played with a pile of small stones. (Moore's hands were never still, and all over his house and studios were piles of objects for the touching: shells, flints, pebbles, crystals.) Two stones accidentally locked, making a perfect fit.

These two incidents, coming close together, were the genesis of the Locking Piece. However, there are always dimmer sources for any work of art—sources less conscious and anecdotal. First there is the artistic readiness, the likelihood of being stimulated by a particular natural observation: This possibility or probability was supplied—for the Locking Piece—by Moore's recurring abstraction, and also by his recurring interest in sculptures made of more than one piece. Another ingredient, perhaps more common in the work of Henry Moore than in the work of most artists, was a connection to his childhood. He remembered, eventually, a device that he had known as a boy, not a locking puzzle but a fireworks toy: You placed a paper cap between two pieces of metal and threw it on the sidewalk to explode. This device fitted together the way the Locking Piece fits.

Sometime in 1962, sitting in the far room at the turntable, Moore made a maquette of the Locking Piece, about four inches tall. In the process of shaping the clay, and turning the small construction about, his hands discovered and created innumerable small reminiscences: the noses, the elephant's foot. If we ask what a nose has to do with an elephant's foot, Moore would answer that all forms are grist to the sculptor's mill: "Likeness is richness," he liked to say. The more a piece contains of different things, Moore believed, the more it would absorb an onlooker. Whatever *is* just what it *is* loses its interest quickly.

"You've got to have some sort of mystery." And different shapes all have meanings: "The way an elephant's foot, soft, will lift up and fall down. It's not the form only. It's all you know of the strength of the elephant too." Form experience brings with it the associations of the form, a vocabulary of feeling and response.

Sometimes after a sculpture was finished, Moore would suddenly come upon new insight into its origins or significance. Perhaps a year after the big Locking Piece was exhibited, and four years after Moore made the original maquette, Julian Huxley invited Moore to his house in Hampstead: There was something Moore had to see. In his garden Huxley had placed, as a sculptural object, the skull of an African elephant—which does not resemble an elephant's foot but closely resembles the Locking Piece itself; the hinge between jaw and skull is the interlocking joint. Moore was delighted; he thought of casting the skull in plaster, to have a copy at Hoglands. As a young man— he remembered—he had seen elephant skulls at museums which he visited in his search for natural forms. Perhaps this recollection provided the final discoverable piece in the mosaic of sources for the Locking Piece.

After Moore made the four-inch maquette, he gave it to his assistants to expand into a version three feet tall. On December 20, 1963, Moore and his helpers were working on the translation of the three-foot figure into the nine-foot final version. This three-part evolution was typical of the process of making Moore's large sculpture. He needed to begin small, with a plaster or clay or plasticine sketch or series of sketches. Enlarging always involved changing, and to go directly from four inches to nine feet (or fourteen feet, or twenty-eight feet) would usually be *too* difficult. The distortions would be so enormous that revisions which might have been made at the three-foot stage would be lost and the sculpture spoiled or abandoned. Often Moore cast all three versions, different as they were. With the Locking Piece, the maquette was never cast because the revisions made for the three-foot version improved it so much.

For these enlargements, Moore gave his assistants a small working model and told them the size he wished the enlargement to become. They covered the model at its extremities with numbers representing the distance from a wooden frame which they moved back and forth over it. Multiplying the distance from a larger frame, they built an armature, nailing together slim pieces of wood and hanging chicken wire from the outermost ends. An armature looks like wire sculpture; if the extremities of wood are numerous, it also looks like a porcupine. They measured the wire of the armature to a point slightly inside the skin of the sculpture-to-be—and then they covered the wire with a thin layer of plaster, while Moore observed their progress and directed revisions. When an assistant copied a maquette or model, constant small questions arose which required Moore's presence for a decision. Revisions in plaster were easily made, but when Isaac Witkin carved an elmwood reclining figure for Moore, he consulted him three or four times a day, since a mistake could have been irrevocable.

The three-foot Locking Piece was cast and exhibited, but Moore intended all along to make the large version. The nine-foot Locking Piece is far more effective than the smaller version. For one thing, size itself is meaningful or expressive. As Moore observed, a mother-and-child figure of life size, or less than life size, makes a tender object. Cast the same pair at thirty feet, and they become terrifying. The Locking Piece is a head only abstractly; instead of becoming terrifying at nine feet, the greater size liberates its facets. The sculpture becomes less a head and more a repository of other forms: The elephant's foot takes on a size fitting its shape, and therefore its associations; landscapes and faces free themselves from the matrix.

The large version is not simply an expansion of the small one. It is always necessary to alter proportions, when you blow up a small sculpture. To begin with, proportions must change even to appear the same, because the new height of the sculpture changes the angle from which the viewer sees it. Also, the twenty-seven-fold increase in volume produced by tripling the dimensions has the effect of making the lines more subtle as well as more monumental. Making the big piece required new decisions, because of new relationships between line and volume. One modification of a line would alter three perspectives, perhaps a nose, a chin, and a mountain. What was convex from one angle might be concave from another, and the shift might be a triumph or a disaster.

One of the admirers of the small Locking Piece was the architect Gordon Bunshaft. Moore told him in October of 1963 that he planned to model a big version, and Bunshaft had the notion that this sculpture would suit a new building of his, the Banque Lambert in Brussels. The Banque owners were interested; however, they wanted to see the Locking Piece *in situ* by the start of February in 1964. Having begun the work in October, Moore could not possibly have had the piece cast and patinated by February; but at least he could, by hurrying, finish a plaster, paint it bronze-color, and transport it to the site for inspection.

To make the large version, Moore's assistants put their measuring marks on the three-foot piece and constructed the large armature. This time the plaster would be too big to cast in one piece; it would have to be sawed into several pieces for casting, so that the armature could contain no nails or wire. They tied the sticks together with ropes, draped cheesecloth from the extremities instead of wire, and applied plaster to the cheesecloth. By December 10, the large Locking Piece looked already finished, a huge white copy of a small bronze original.

But it was not finished. Work had fallen behind because bad weather had kept Moore from rolling the sculpture outside to have a good look at it. It was impossible to make crucial discriminations inside the studio, where he could stand only a few feet from the plaster. Today Moore and his assistants opened the big shed doors and pushed the Locking Piece onto the concrete, wedging crowbars under its wooden platform. The white shape dazzled in the winter sun. For two hours Moore studied it from all angles and distances. His assistants moved it around full circle, a few inches at a time, and moved the three-foot model along with it. They shifted a plain cardboard background to cut off interference from other bronzes outside the studio. After Moore had stared hard at the two Locking Pieces from each new angle, he started giving directions for revision of the new one—

sometimes making rapid pencil sketches in a notebook while Isaac Witkin looked over his shoulder. Ron Swan stood to one side, listening, not speaking.

The language was simple. "We need to take the wobble out of our line." "If we have that bit curved out that way, don't you think it makes it difficult to join it to that piece up there? We have to curve it *in*, so that it will make a join for that other piece up there." "That's a flat surface. It's going over *that* way too much." "That we were talking about before as being too curved, it's too curved from here too." "This gets wider, you see, and I wanted it to. I want it to look as if it gets wider all the way to the top. This one gets narrower." "Go down on that side and file it down there." "Our curve at the top there isn't flat enough. This corner wants to go higher. That is, this should go off straighter here, before it begins to curve."

There was much talk about weak and strong. "Take the calipers to the little bronze and then to the big one, and see if it comes out three times. It looks too weak to me." "Doesn't that piece down there, that is holding up the locking joint, look a bit weak? Like a thin milk bottle?" There were other comparisons to objects, especially to faces. "That lower part of the lip there." "The chin is weak." Between Henry Moore and Isaac Witkin there was immediate understanding. Moore's hand drew a quick stroke with a ballpoint pen down a sheet of lined note paper, and Witkin assented, "Yes, yes." The eye not the mind appeared to do the judging. Making formal decisions, Moore's face lost its affable charm; his eyes brightened and his face became concentrated and intense. Sometimes Moore bounded up to the plaster itself, and taking a long stick pointed to a protuberance or a hollow, talking in little bursts. With his sporty checks and his long stick he looked like Don Quixote as a country gentleman.

"It's not easy. It's not easy," Moore kept saying, between his corrections. When the big sculptures-in-process remained outside all the time in the summer, these conferences went on several times a day, and work would go faster than it did in the winter. "Sometimes you have to carry a curve really far out before you know that it's wrong. Another part gets finished that changes things." Today the sun was bright and looked warm, but everyone was stamping his feet to keep his toes from freezing. Though it was not long past noon, the low winter sun cast the manlike shadow of the Glenkiln Cross across the grass. "This in here looks a little *too* round and that will make it narrower." By one o'clock, the Locking Piece had been shifted around on its small wheels until it had returned to its original place. "Our shape isn't quite right here, in the face, in the nose here. It looks to me as if it should be a little wider at the bottom. The biggest width should be low down, not in the middle. That is, there would be more *weight* down here. Well, there we are. Let's call it a morning's work." The assistants decided to leave the piece outside, to begin work in the open air after lunch. It would take them three or four days to follow out the morning's directions.

Lunch was on the sun porch again, boiled gammon, potatoes and cabbage. Sheila cooked it, and her simple lunches are the Moores' main meal. Before Sheila came to work, the Moores sometimes lacked a main meal. If Irina was absorbed in gardening, Henry would suggest boiled eggs or cheese and crackers for lunch. Things were more regular now, with a hot meal at noon and a cold plate at night—perhaps potted shrimps or cold chicken or cheese or sliced beef. In London, where they ate at least once a week, the Moores often treated themselves to the Cafe Royal on Regent Street near Piccadilly Circus.

Moore seemed pleased with the morning's work and chatted lightly among the women who surrounded him, Irina and Mary and Mrs. Tinsley. He ate quickly, talking between bites, and when he finished his pudding, rested for a few minutes in the small, old living room at the front of the house. After the addition of the new wing, this became the telly room, where the Moores spent many evenings watching "Coronation Street" and "Z Cars." In the daytime the room was cold and dark but relieved by a wood fire and the presence of works of art—primitives and Henry Moores. As Moore talked sleepily after lunch, a ten-minute talking nap, his hands idly caressed a bronze maquette, and shifted to a pebble, and moved again to an old wooden stringed figure of his own.

Then abruptly he stood, stretched and strode out to the far room again, to work some more on waxes. The room had warmed up to 60 degrees and the wax was more malleable, but it was dark at two o'clock, and Moore switched on the fluorescent lamp fixed to the ceiling. Night would fall in two hours— in December in England—and now he would not notice its coming. With another strip of paper ignited at the electric fire, he started the alcohol lamp burning again and set to work. For an hour there was no interruption. In the house Mrs. Tinsley typed letters and fought off the telephone. Outside the studio five hundred yards away Isaac Witkin and Ron Swan in the premature twilight added and subtracted plaster from the Locking Piece. Moore worked over one wax and then another, finishing neither. Then there was a knock at the door; Mrs. Tinsley apologized, but the *New York Times* was calling from London and absolutely insisted that she speak to him. "They want to know if they can photograph the Lincoln Center Reclining Figure," which Moore had stopped work on, temporarily, in order to finish the Locking Piece.

"No."

"I told them I was sure they couldn't."

"Tell them it's in the agreement."

"They want to know how far along it is, and they want to interview you about it. They want to talk with you now."

Moore looked perplexed and irritated, not wanting to refuse and not wanting to interrupt his work. "Tell them I'm in a mix of plaster," he said as he returned to his waxes.

Another hour went by undisturbed. A wax was finished and put in the box with the two finished that morning. Then Mrs. Tinsley returned. Gordon Bunshaft was on the phone from New York; he had consulted the owners of the Banque Lambert in Brussels and was able to give Moore one extra week on the Locking Piece. Moore was elated; now he felt *sure* he could finish the piece and have it in Brussels on time. And now was a good moment to break for tea.

Tea was in the big dining room at the front of the house, where the Moores had breakfasted eight hours before. Flowers filled the center of the table, and Irina poured tea for Henry and Mrs. Tinsley. There was a cake, which Irina had bought at a church sale in Much Hadham, and a plate of cookies. Conversation picked up from lunch. Mary returned from town halfway through tea and quickly became center of attention. The phone rang in the office and Mrs. Tinsley left the table to answer it. It was a telegram from Australia that requested the "world's greatest sculptor" to design a monument in Sydney. Moore would refuse the commission but smiled happily at the phrase.

After tea Moore worked another half-hour on a wax and put it away in the box with the others. The day counted four waxes finished, as well as a large step forward on the Locking Piece. Then he reluctantly turned off the lights and the heaters in the far room, locked the door, and spent an hour dictating urgent letters. Mrs. Tinsley went home, and an old friend arrived from London to show Moore a 1932 drawing, a sketch for sculpture which the friend had bought at an auction. Moore remembered making the drawing, and the two of them talked about it while they had a drink in the new living room. The wing was added in 1960, a room and bath for Mary above it. The living room's floor shines with a gold carpet, and on the walls are a variety of paintings: a Cezanne cartoon for The Bathers, an explosive painting by Alan Davie, the figure of an angel from a Renaissance church. Standing in a niche near the ceiling there were three leaf figures by Henry Moore.

After half an hour Irina and Mary joined Moore and his old friend, and after another half-hour the friend left to return to London. For supper, on trays in front of the telly, the Moores moved back to the old living room, and watched television until 9:30, when Henry drove Mary to her dance. Since someone else was bringing her back, he went home to bed and slept. The huge white shape of the Locking Piece, altered since he saw it last, shimmered faintly in the glass-topped studio at the end of the garden.

It was not a typical day, but no day is typical. Sometimes Moore fidgeted in London all day, sitting on a committee, going to a show, visiting a bronze foundry. In summer he traveled back and forth between his old studios and his new ones on a bicycle. Many days, afternoons were interrupted by visitors whom he showed around with courtesy, explaining things for the hundredth time without boredom. Visitors ranged from a single collector or art critic to busloads of students. Sometimes in the evening he sketched, not drawing for exhibition but letting his pencil idly scribble forms across the page, not knowing himself what he would do next. Other evenings, if the mood was on him, he would sit in the far room with a piece of clay and try to make a new shape, a shape that in a few months might rear in the ghost-white of plaster in a big new studio at the bottom of the garden.

Weekends were a different routine. Saturday mornings were Irina's time out. The Moores drove to Bishop's Stortford late Saturday morning and went shopping. At one o'clock they had lunch at the Foxley Hotel. Home by 2:30, they received the Saturday visitors. Sunday at home was quiet, and Sunday morning was often Moore's *best* time for work. If the work didn't go well, he felt awful: "I'm terribly sad, remembering childhood when we could have no pleasure on Sunday. It's a Puritan northern feeling, that Sunday feeling." But mostly early on Sunday he worked well, and he looked forward to Sunday morning all week. The assistants were not there, there were no phone calls from architects or newspapers, there was no mail, no Mrs. Tinsley, and no photographers—nothing but silent studios and the world of forms.

Moore put the final touches to his Locking Piece on Sunday morning, January 26, 1964. The assistants had done their last work the day before, painting the plaster a realistic bronze-color, but Moore enjoyed being alone with it, touching it, making little changes. Monday the 27th the truck came for it, one of those huge low-loaders which usually carry heavy road equipment. A crane, built into a separate truck, lifted the sculpture onto the low-loader, and it started its journey to Brussels. When it arrived the plaster had cracked and Isaac Witkin flew over to mend it. It was sited, admired, accepted by the owners of the Banque Lambert, and departed for Berlin to be cast. (Moore's Berlin founder had the equipment to cast big bronzes; Moore used English founders for most smaller sculptures.) As the low-loader was crossing the border into West Germany, the drivers discovered that the Locking Piece was cracking badly again, and they refused to drive further. Agents from the founder arrived and packed the pieces into wooden cases, and when the dismembered parts arrived in West Berlin, Isaac Witkin took another European journey—reassembling the Locking Piece like a three-dimensional jigsaw puzzle.

COUSY'S FIRES

It is a large and comfortable house on Salisbury Street in Worcester, with land enough for privacy, behind a stone wall next to a Catholic academy. Bob Cousy opens the door and beckons us in. This April Saturday he wears a running suit, electric blue with a white stripe, and his bare feet lounge in slippers. His hair is gray now—it is 1985 as I meet him; he is fifty-six years old—and this aging athlete is slim as a trout and quick as a fox. When he labored for the Boston Celtics from 1950 to 1964, Bob Cousy was the best playmaker in the NBA; some call him the best ever. His game was clever, sudden, intelligent, and innovative. He improvised the impossible play; he looked left and drove right, then threw the ball accurately to a teammate behind him who flashed to the basket. I remember my early astonishment, sitting in the old Boston Arena in 1948 or 1949—Cousy and I were born the same year, college students at the same time—as I watched the sharp-featured Holy Cross undergraduate dribble behind his back. He was not the first to do so, but for many of us—in those years of the two-handed set shot—Cousy was the original dazzler of the hardwood floor.

He dazzled for the Celtics fourteen green years, ending with five world championships in a row. *Only* fourteen years: An athlete's "garland"—as A. E. Housman liked to put it—is "briefer than a girl's." The Chief Executive Officer of Megacorp keeps driving for the basket until he reaches retirement age; so does the composer of electronic music and the building contractor—but Cousy stopped dribbling basketballs at the age of thirty-five. The passion that drove him to excellence drove him out of the game. When he no longer *wanted* the ball for the final shot, it was time to retire.

Cousy was not only brilliant; he was also the world's most competitive man, possessed of the killer instinct, as he calls it. When he muses about his old violence, his feelings are complex. Because this instinct fueled the engine that made him what he was, he owes everything to it—yet he is *embarrassed* to have felt homicidal over a boy's game. By nature reflective and ironic, Bob Cousy left civilization behind when the buzzer sounded: The fox grew long eyeteeth and turned into a wolf. Not that he was a physical player, as the euphemism has it. At six-foot-two he was often the smallest of ten combatants, but smallest in size was often largest in concentration or obsession. Before big games he isolated himself, building the anxiety and tension that fed his skill. His stomach gave him trouble; he suffered pains in his chest. ("I've had more EKGs than any man alive.") After brooding in a rage of preparation and pain, he exploded in a perfection of skill and maneuver.

After retirement the fires of competition raged their worst. At first he coached for Boston College, wanting to win as much as ever, but without a physical outlet for his killer instinct. He tells a story of meeting his players' parents, before the first game of the season, doubled over with anxious stomach pain. ("What kind of a coach is *this*?") Always in the summer, at his basketball camp in New Hampshire, he suffered from nightmares. A sleepwalker as a child, now in middle-age he rocketed out of bed, dead-asleep, screaming at dream-pursuers, ran outdoors pell-mell and crashed running into his own automobile; he raced toward the lake with his wife Missie in vain pursuit. He woke up confused, bruised, ribs fractured, burned by vain fires.

He sits on a soft sofa now, telling with irony and humor about his old violence, an urbane Reynard making light of old passions. What tinder and what flint started this burning?

Like many athletes, Bob Cousy grew up poor, born just after his parents emigrated to this country. ("I was *fabriqué en France*.") He ran the streets of Manhattan's East Side during the Depression, his father a New York cabby who moonlighted a second job. When he was twelve years old the family scraped money together to buy a house on Long Island. The Cousys lived in cellar and attic, renting out the more agreeable middle floors, struggling to survive poverty and each other. His tall mother and tiny father fought day and night. (He wonders if his father worked long hours not only to feed his family but to get out of the house.) In a fierce mother and a quiet hard-working father, Bob Cousy found a double model of heat and diligence.

Diligent fires burn gently now: no more nightmares, fewer stomachaches and EKGs. Instead of ulcers and coronaries he accumulates an estate. When he retired from basketball Cousy had fame, a bad stomach, and no savings. After his years at BC, he coached the professional team in Cincinnati, and the job paid well because the Cousy name sold tickets.

When he left coaching, the name also generated PR jobs—"soft PR"—a round of golf with a CEO, telling "a few silly stories." And now, for his name and for his able words, Bob Cousy performs as color-man on Boston television broadcasts of Celtics road games. A born teacher, he educates his listeners patiently and without condescension, providing clear insights in lively language salted with irony. If he is partisan, as local commentators are obliged to be, he is never blatant. Cousy would be superb (and objective) for national broadcasts, were it not for his strong and eccentric Worcester/Long Island accent, combined with a slight impediment, gathered around the letter r, which leads him to describe maneuvers like the "lunning lighthander."

The house in Worcester is a rich man's ("It is our one extravagance") paid for by twenty years of a private fellow's public appearances. By the time he turns sixty, he hopes to withdraw from the public life.* "There is a time," he says, "for banking fires." There is also a time for improvising new interests: Earlier, Cousy never had time to learn to play the piano; now he takes weekly lessons and practices daily. Although he is not content unless he is physically active, he is now satisfied by golf and tennis with old friends in Worcester. It has been years ("Thank goodness!") since he has thrown a club in anger.

No hoop dangles over the Cousy garage, and he rarely

---

*At sixty-five he still broadcasts for the Celtics.

touches a basketball. (A hoop hung there for his daughters when they were little, not for him—until Assumption College students scavenged it three years back.) He has largely refused invitations to old-timers' games, for the retired master will not mock his old skills, but in 1985 he succumbed to two old-timer invitations, first at a celebration for his old coach Red Auerbach, then at an NBA affair in support of professionals who retired before the pension plan. He prepared himself by shooting baskets and working out at a college gym in Worcester. Old-timers' games resemble twenty-fifth reunions, as paunchy old boys whoop it up by rehearsing green days: "We have heard the chimes at midnight, Master Shallow." There's a sadness to all reunions, and on the basketball floor the diminished motions of middle age italicize youth's loss. After the Celtics' old-boy game, a reporter quoted Cousy: "I worked out for a month for this game. I got feeling pretty good. I tried to make a fancy move." The reporter asked, "What did the doctor say?" "Just a pulled hamstring," said Cousy.

Listening to this middle-aged man—agreeable, ironic, sophisticated—I remember the wiry fellow I glimpsed almost forty years ago when we were in college. Of course I wonder if the killer instinct can feel content in a comfortable home playing comfortable tennis and comfortable golf, wolf studying the role of senior citizen. So I ask: "Are you content?" This supple shape in blue running suit, reticent man who has performed his charm in twenty-thousand interviews, stops smiling for a moment. Fifty-six-year-old eyes grow sharp. "Reasonably," he says.

Surely the qualification is accurate: Cousy knows that life is neither simple or easy. If you are as clever as you are lucky, if you are as shrewd as you are hard-working, you may—tentatively, knock on wood—achieve reasonable contentment.

Like all men and women of ambition Bob Cousy lives with regrets. His regrets remind me of Carl Yaztremski's and Robert Frost's, and of laments pronounced by leading executives and politicians: All successful people understand, in middle life, that they missed out on the childhood of their children because they were intent on pursuing their own ambitions. Bob Cousy shakes his head remembering how his two daughters grew up: "Shhh. Daddy is taking a nap before the game." Ambitious people compensate by fawning over the next generation. Lately the old playmaker has become a grandfather, and the first grandchild resides in Seattle. "Buy airline stock," says Bob Cousy.

AUERBACH IN BRONZE

A few years ago,* the City of Boston erected a statue of Red Auerbach in the Faneuil Hall Marketplace near the effigy of James Michael Curley, another shrewd benefactor of Boston, once re-elected mayor while serving a term in jail. In his latest hurrah, the bronze creator of the Boston Celtics sits on a bench upright and alert; fans and tourists sit beside him to get their pictures taken. He carries a clenched program in his left hand; its ring finger sports the jewels of the NBA Championship. In his right hand he clasps an enormous bronze cigar, fondled so much by tourists and fans that it shines like St. Peter's toe.

In 1986, at the behest of a magazine called *Sport*, I visited the statue's original, in his aging flesh. I made my report:

Red Auerbach keeps a large and cluttered den on Causeway Street, in Celtics offices that connect by a bridge of sighs to the great leaky ark of Boston Garden. As I enter the office, the first thing that greets me is a lifelike cardboard cutout of Red Auer-

---

*Written in 1986, this piece includes anachronisms. Corrections would outdate themselves soon enough.

bach smiling and gesturing—a two-dimensional replica which I start to address. As I recognize my error and turn to the real man, the telephone rings and Auerbach answers it. While I sit facing the man, his cardboard image hovers over my right ear; one Red Auerbach talks into a telephone, and I swivel my head to find another Red Auerbach looking down at me.

While the man speaks with somebody about giving a lecture, I do a room-inventory. The glorious junk of a lifetime overflows this room. On the walls hundreds of photographs mostly picture tall young men wearing shorts: family pictures of the multitudinous sons. Then I count at least twenty caricatures of the father figure himself. On the desk, on a table, and on shelves extending from a wall are dozens of letter-openers from Auerbach's extensive and global collection: blades that look like steel, ivory, pewter, bronze; handles of ivory, gold, cloisonné, enamel. (Later I find that most of his letter-opener collection stays in Washington, D.C., where Auerbach has retained residence while commuting to Boston over thirty-six years.) On the wall hangs a jacket from the Washington Caps, Auerbach's first team as a professional coach in 1946. There are framed citations, trophies galore, mementos that look like toys for grownups (a small cannon, a boomerang, basketball dolls), a painting that ennobles Jo Jo White, plants, books, and sculptures that look African and Oriental.

He hangs up and we talk. In July of 1986 Arnold Red Auerbach has come north to Boston for the first time since his latest sports injury. Playing tennis earlier in the month, this septuagenarian leapt for a ball like Larry Bird (whom he beat on the courts five years ago; "How can you let yourself be beaten by a sixty-five-year-old man?" taunted Auerbach) and laid himself up. "I dove for the ball. Boris Becker! A poor man's Boris Becker! I just dove flat out for it, got the ball back; and tried to roll over . . . *Bang!* I hit the deck and broke two ribs." It is noted that he got the ball back; it is noted that he lets me *know* that he got the ball back. This is the same ancient fellow who, three years ago in exhibition season, lost his temper and assaulted Moses Malone. When I remind him he laughs. "Billy Cunningham called me up the next day. 'Goddamn!' he says. 'You never change!' " As he laughs the lines that ray from his eyes deepen, and for a moment he looks like a man in his seventieth year. He sits slightly stooped, his once red hair a sparse gray. His physical self seems shrunken, or at least it feels smaller than the whole presence of the man. But the energy he exudes—even lounging back in his chair speaking mildly—removes the wrinkles one by one until his age is invisible.

Red Auerbach intends to work out three times a week—"Racquetball; tennis, something to get a little sweat up . . ."—but he no longer challenges his players at horse. "As you get older," he acknowledges with a sigh, "the ball gets heavier." I remember Auerbach's former all-star Bob Cousy, eleven years younger than the coach, who meditates now on "banking the fires of competition." If you are unable to cool down the flames, they burn the lining of your stomach. When I mention Cousy's endeavor, Auerbach nods his head. Leaning back in his chair, puffing at his logo, surrounded by trophies of the life lived, he speaks softly: "It's just *age*," he says. "You've got to learn to adjust to the limitations. It's difficult. You *try* to keep up the fire . . ." I realize that, unlike his old point guard, Auerbach struggles with match and kerosene not with firehose. (Cousy is not president of the Boston Celtics.) "But you find that you need, oh, a little more rest . . . a little more away-time." He blows out a great enveloping blue cloud. "If you don't have that driving interest, it's transmitted to the coaches and players; they *feel* it."

He has been speaking almost dreamily, in a soft voice rather high in the register, milder and more reflective than I had expected. In his autobiography he called himself an introvert, which startled me until I realized that everybody, even the wildest public man, knows in his secret heart that he is an introvert. (When I questioned him about the word, he explained: "It's a guy that likes his own privacy." All celebrities confide to interviewers: "I am a very private person.") Suddenly he blasts me out of my chair with a booming horn of a voice, as he looks past me to the corridor outside. His voice drops eight octaves and rises two hundred decibels; his accent becomes street-Brooklyn, like Archie in the old "Duffy's Tavern": "*Hey! M. L.! Don't go away!*"

Turning my head I see, leaning gracefully against a door-jamb, the tall and elegant form of M. L. Carr, who played in the Celtics backcourt from 1979 to 1985, when age slowed him down and he was let go. Apparently M. L. started to enter the boss's office but noticed a visitor; as I catch sight of him he pirouettes lightly, stylish as Barishnikov and dressed to the nines in polished shoes, crisply creased gray flannels, green blazer, white shirt, and striped tie. He tilts his head back to regard Auerbach who bellows again: "*M. L.! Don't go away!*"

M. L. adopts a studied look of puzzlement and speaks in a teasing, high-pitched, pondering voice: "Now that's *interesting*, you tell me that . . . A year ago, you told me to go away!"

Red Auerbach laughs. "OK," he says. "Go away but don't stay away."

As it happens, this old off-guard and friend—not a great star but a useful character-actor in the Celtics repertory company—exemplifies Auerbach's shrewd abilities in casting. (He should be called not General Manager or President but Artistic Director.) Michael Leon Carr's career with the Celtics was Go Away But Don't Stay Away. After Carr played a little in the ABA, the Celtics tried him out as a free agent in 1974, but he didn't make the club; then he played in Israel; then he played in the Eastern Basketball Association . . . In 1976, M. L. Carr stuck with the Detroit Pistons; in 1979 he made the most steals in the NBA, and Auerbach was ready for him. He came to the Celtics from the Detroit Pistons in compensation for Detroit's free-agent signing of Bob McAdoo; he came in addition to two first-round choices Auerbach dealt to Golden State, and eventually had turned *one* aging offense-only center into *three* players named Carr, Parish, and McHale.

M. L. Carr played out his career with the Celtics and contributed especially on defense to the championship teams of 1981 and 1984. The other pair remained to start for the 1986 champions. We may remind ourselves that on the 1986 team, all five starters came to the Celtics by eccentric routes. In 1978 everybody knew that Larry Bird was a player; but only the Celtics drafted him as a future when he had a year of college eligibility left. When the Celtics named him in the second round in 1981, Danny Ainge was a good-field/no-hit third-baseman for the Toronto Bluejays. In 1983 Phoenix traded Dennis Johnson to Boston straight up for Rick Robey, whom they released three years later.

We all know whose shrewdness assembled this team. For twenty years Frenchified sportswriters, talking about the Boston Celtics, have gone to Larousse to spell *mystique*, easily the most overworked Gallicism since *Chevrolet coupe*. Dissidents have been quick to repair the orthography: R-u-s-s-e-l-l in one era, and B-i-r-d in another. But the true orthography—in one era and out the other—is A-u-e-r-b-a-c-h, and there has never been another such institution in American sports: In sixteen years as a coach he won nine championships; in thirty-six years of running the show, he has collected sixteen.

Red Auerbach is the most dominant single figure in the history of American professional sport. The New York Yankees for decades dominated the American League in baseball but no one coach or general manager or owner could be accused of responsibility.

Houdini—or Diaghilev or Peter Sellars or Thomas Alva Edison—began life in Brooklyn in 1917, son of an immigrant from Minsk who worked his way to owning a dry-cleaning establishment. (Auerbach still presses his own trousers on occasion at a friend's shop; it takes him back.) His father Hymie's character, Auerbach says, differed from his own: "Everybody *liked* him." He admires his father and like many men who admire their fathers he admires *fatherhood*. To his team he has been protective, fair, difficult, tender, demanding, and, above all, paternal.

Although he admires his father's easy popularity, he made good use of his own abrasiveness: "At first I didn't like Red Auerbach," says a rival coach, "but in time I grew to hate him." If you spend energy hating Red Auerbach, maybe you do not play so well against him: To this day, Wilt Chamberlain will not say his name aloud.

In street and schoolyard young Auerbach became an athlete, as sport provided exit from Brooklyn to college by way of scholarship. His ability as a basketball player was "mostly in my head." A point guard and passer, he was "a good defensive player. I could maintain my concentration." Second-team all-Brooklyn, an achievement for which some of his Celtics teased him, he attended Seth Low Junior College and transferred to finish at George Washington University.

His potential as a pro was not an issue in 1940, when he could pick up twenty dollars maybe by driving to Wilkes-Barre to play semi-pro. He had majored in physical education in order to become a teacher and a coach. After college—team captain his senior year, high scorer—he picked up his M.A. at G.W. while coaching at St. Albans Prep in Washington. He worked for the city on playgrounds, refereed, and then taught American history while coaching at a Washington high school. An early academic triumph was the publication of an article in *The Journal of Health and Physical Education* in March 1943 on the construction and utility of indoor obstacle courses. (High school students trained for combat in 1943.) In 1986 in his office on

Causeway Street, Red Auerbach reaches into a bookshelf and hands me the *Journal* opened to his learned paper. "I had the centerfold, see? 'A. J. Auerbach, Roosevelt High School, Washington.'" Even when you are sixty-nine, and there is a statue of you downstreet, you take pride in the by-line that glorified your twenty-sixth year.

After three years in the wartime Navy as an instructor in physical education, Auerbach began his professional career in 1946, coaching the Washington Caps of the newly founded Basketball Association of America. In 1950 he came to the Boston Celtics, hired by Walter Brown who owned the team and was losing money. In recent years a ticket has been hard to come by; it was not always so. When the Celtics with Bill Russell at center won eleven championships in thirteen years, they sold out only for playoffs—and New Englanders missed watching great teams they would now pawn their ancestors to see. Basketball was for New York, Kentucky, and Indiana; in the North country hockey was the sport. Boys skated, bashing each other, and some high schools never even assembled a basketball team. I went to Hamden High in Connecticut where the student body regularly watched hockey games en masse, rioting in support like English soccer crowds. For basketball, maybe twenty-five relatives and girlfriends assembled to watch our set-shooters who towered as high as five-foot-seven and generally lost 39–23.

The New England exception was Holy Cross, and chauvinist sportswriters ignorant of basketball made a shrine of Holy Cross—1947 NCAA champs who boasted a 27–4 record in 1949–50. That spring when Red Auerbach, at his first news conference as Celtics coach, was asked if he would draft the great Holy Cross senior Bob Cousy, he referred to the demigod as a "local yokel." Enemies he made in that moment hectored him for decades. Later, in order to stop an idiot chorus claiming that Holy Cross could beat the Celtics, Auerbach scheduled a scrimmage—with predictable results that silenced the morons.

Then Cousy by an improbable series of accidents found himself dumped on the Celtics and Red Auerbach, fortunately for the Celtics and for Red Auerbach. Fortunately for Cousy also. Before he proved himself, basketball people had feared that his brilliant style of play was out of control. When he teamed up with Bill Sharman the Celtics backcourt was superb, but the team lacked size (and championships) until in 1956 the Celtics signed Tom Heinsohn, from Holy Cross, and Auerbach dealt two players to St. Louis in order to draft Bill Russell. Russell's rebounding allowed the Boston Celtics, Cousy and all, to rise to the top and stay there.

By 1986 things have changed. The Celtics have sold out every game at the Garden since 19 December 1980. If you know someone in the Celtics hierarchy, your pull may allow you to *buy* a ticket. Even rural New England is crazy for Auerbach's Celtics. I live in the New Hampshire countryside and on Sunday mornings at the South Danbury Church we warm up for the service by bragging about what the Celtics did last week. Annie Walker has played the organ on and off for sixty years. "How do you like our boys?" asks Annie on Sunday morning after the Celtics win their twelfth in a row.

Auerbach's notions about roundball were set long ago. He praises his coach from George Washington, Bill Reinhart, and he repeats the theme that the game has not changed. Bodies get taller and quicker but the game is the same. "I was always a fundamentalist. Like my book." He refers to *Basketball for the Players, the Fan, and the Coach*. "It's in seven languages. It was written in 1952. Most of it is applicable to today's game."

He has not always favored innovations. Twenty years ago he was vehement against the suggestion that the NBA install a three-point shot. "I was wrong," he says quickly. But many modern wrinkles in the game are Auerbach's own, tried out, not in practice or even at rookie camp, but on schoolyards during Washington summers. When Auerbach relaxes from professional basketball there is nothing he likes so much as to watch basketball. "I go to watch high school. Even today, it's nothing for me to go watch a summer league. I go out to Maryland, or Georgetown, or George Washington, and I watch teams practice. Just for relaxation." Well, not only: "Some of the best plays I ever devised were at Sunday mornings on the playgrounds. We'd get there early, guys like Elgin Baylor, Dave Bing, guys around Washington, even as professionals, working out on a Sunday morning in the playground during the summer. Sometimes I'd get there a little early, and I'd say: 'Look, I've got an idea.' If we could do it on the playground, we could do it in the NBA. That's where I invented all those out-of-bounds plays, when people line up across the street."

He stubs his cigar out in an abundant ashtray. From time to time he glances into the corridor; I expect a Valhalla of Celtics Past to pirouette in the doorway. I ask: "Do they keep coming back, like M. L.?" He nods: He is happy that the sons return; they grow potbellies and gray hair but they are sons and they return. "I talked to Ramsay just two days ago. I know where *every one* of them is. Gene Conley down the street, Finkel, Kuberski, Satch, Havlicek. When they're not around, I talk to them; I talk to McCauley; I even see Bones McKinney now and then." Bones McKinney was a 1946 acquisition for Auerbach's Washington Caps, who played for the Celtics late in his career. Although Bill Russell lives in Seattle, "I see him all the time because he works for TBS. I see his daughter all the time. She's at Harvard Law School. I see her all the time."

In a moment he walks around the desk to the great humidor of cigars, to pick out another one. He offers me one which I refuse; then I change my mind: I pick one out and cherish it into an inside jacket pocket. Maybe I can bronze it, like the cigar the statue smokes.

Auerbach's affection for Bill Russell turns up continually as he speaks, and when he talks about the particulars of basketball his examples are Bill Russell first. "Who is the best athlete you ever coached?" He will list Cousy, Sharman, and Gene Conley who played major league baseball and basketball at the same time; but first he will say: "Russell was a great athlete." Even more than his athletic ability, it is Russell's integrity and brainpower that Auerbach returns to again and again. Integrity, or frequently the want of it, is an Auerbach theme. There is a tolerable difference for Auerbach between doing everything to win a game—everything legal—and going back on your word. He is old-fashioned and upright about handshakes and agreements. "Integrity" and "brightness"—both attributes of Bill Russell— salt his speech. "He is very bright, Russell, *very bright*."

There are other favorites, even outside basketball. His

daughter Randy works for Mel Brooks. Mel Brooks has become an Auerbach crony: "I went over there with Larry Bird one time, and he entertained us for an hour and a half!" He laughs and shakes his head; he cannot provide examples. Brooks is a *good* man, he tells me, who cares for people around him. Then he adds, "He's not only funny he's *bright.*"

When Bill Russell succeeded Auerbach as coach of the Celtics, on Auerbach's retirement in 1966, he became the first black head coach in the history of American professional sports. The piece of history approaches a sore point. I talked with Bob Cousy a week before seeing his old mentor, and Cousy handed me a ticking package: Joking, he suggested that I ask Arnold (as Cousy likes to call him) if the Celtics had instituted a quota system. Predictably, Arnold glowers: "He's kidding," he says.

There are many ways to hate the Boston Celtics. In the 1980s, a prestigious form of Celtic-hatred became disapproval of their pale lineup. Residents of monochrome suburbs shook their heads noticing that grayboys formed seven-elevenths of the Celtics' team; Knicks fans who lived behind doormen on Sutton Place deplored the Celtics for starting three whites out of five; Los Angeles film producers driving DeLoreans regretted the irrefutable fact that the Celtics could play five whites not including Larry Bird and Kevin McHale. Never in the history of America was so much civil-rights fervor expended in the service of athletic partisanship by so many rich white folks.

Any ground for suspicion lies not in Celtics history but in the city where the Celtics practice their craft. Boston is infamous for its historic racism and so are its Red Sox. But Auerbach's record is clear. Here is an NBA race-quiz: Which team in the National Basketball Association was the first to draft a black player? Which was the first to start five black players? Which was the first to hire a black coach? One name answers all three questions.

Auerbach refuses to take credit. If you take credit for playing blacks you must take blame for not playing them. "It's all crap! If a guy can do a job we don't care about his color. *It just happens!*"

I expected Red Auerbach to be shrewd, smart, and competitive; he is all these things—and he is softer than I expected, less harsh, and more of an aesthete, even as an observer of basketball. The fast break is his favorite occupation—but for the beauty of it, his favorite play is the pick and roll: "It has to be timed *just so*; the guy with the ball has to make a decision whether to go, to shoot, or to pass." As he speaks his hands gesture and he smiles with something like tenderness; he is like a gourmet describing the best omelette he ever ate, or a theatre-lover the best Hedda Gabler. Red Auerbach loves precision of execution—in basketball, in tennis, in baseball, and in letter-openers.

For twenty years and more, Auerbach spent part of each summer in Europe, Africa, and Asia, generally accompanied by a tall assistant, to give clinics and spread the word about the American game, NBA version. He loved these trips, sponsored by the United States Information Agency of the State Department. From time to time he took Don Nelson with him, Bill

Russell of course, John Havlicek, Tom Heinsohn, Bob Cousy—
to Japan, to Taiwan, to Burma, to Bangkok, and all over Africa.
Wherever he went, he held his clinics in the morning—so that
in the afternoon he could shop. "I bought silver, ivory, cloisonné . . . I know *a lot* about that stuff." After teacher Auerbach
held morning clinics in basketball for citizens of Bangkok, in
the afternoon he taught silver, ivory, and cloisonné to a large
companion.

I ask him: "Is your Washington house full of this stuff?"

He nods his head smiling; it is another happiness, like his
continuing friendship with old players.

"*Unbelievable!*" he says.

Red Auerbach's two daughters grew up in Washington among
the unbelievable possessions—but largely in the absence of
their father. Auerbach's team-family took precedence over the
family of flesh. These days he sees more of his real family—and
he wants them to have things *now*, not after he is dead—but continually he argues with himself about the years of separation.
"If anybody ever tries to tell you that they are not affected at
home by what happens on the court, they're lousy coaches. Bad
as it was, being away from my family, it was a blessing in disguise. Most coaches with their wives are relatively unhappy."

He still flies to Boston for many home games, and listens in
Washington on a radio hookup to the rest, hearing the redoubt-
able Johnny Most, greatest Homer since the blind poet. He also
leaves the District to lecture, maybe three or four times a month.
Sometimes he talks for bread and butter, as he did last night

down at the Cape, talking to a convention of cable television people; often he talks for charities; he lectures at Harvard five times a year, a class in sports law given by Professors Weiler and Dershowitz.

Every summer he comes to Boston for rookie camp, which this year enacts itself at Brandeis University in Waltham, and at the same time he runs his own one-week basketball camp—with college players as counselors. The Celtics first-round draft choice in 1986, Len Bias was a counselor at Auerbach's camp for three years, which was how Auerbach came to know and cherish him. The death of Len Bias—a cocaine overdose—the day after he was drafted as a Celtic, is the hardest thing that Auerbach has endured in his basketball years. It is the only true darkness I feel in this man. When I mention Len Bias I feel like a ghoul.

As I prepare to leave, I ask Red Auerbach a final question which I keep to the end because I figure that I won't get anywhere with it. In a sense I don't, because it is the only question that makes him impatient. I ask: "Do you think about dying?" Red Auerbach sweeps his hand to push the question away: "I don't want to go into that. That gets morbid." At the same time, he answers my question: He asks, "Have you seen that statue?"

Before I get to the door, the bullhorn voice starts up behind me: "*M. L.! M. L!*"

OCTOBER'S SHORTSTOP

As we waited for the World Series of 1968, most of us concentrated on a matchup of pitchers. Detroit's Dennis McLain, thirty-one and six on the season—the first pitcher to win thirty games since Dizzy Dean in 1934—would go against the Cardinals' Bob Gibson, whose nifty powerful kick gave him the handsomest motion in baseball. But the matchup fizzled. Gibson pitched very well—three complete games, two and one, with an ERA of 1.67—but McLain lost two, winning only the sixth game when the Tigers came up with ten runs in the third inning. After the favored Cardinals lost in seven games, it was a portly biker named Mickey Lolich who had pitched the Tigers to three victories.

Lolich was glorious, but many baseball people felt that the Tigers won because their manager made one of the weirdest strategic moves in baseball history. Mayo Smith switched his centerfielder—a twenty-six-year-old, in his third year with the Tigers, a high-school pitcher turned minor league outfielder— to play baseball's most demanding position besides the battery: Mickey Stanley started all seven games at shortstop.

By 1968 I had lived ten years in Michigan, and I had come around to Detroit's baseball club in its small antiquated beautiful Tiger Stadium—a baseball park as fine as Fenway Park or Wrigley Field, but without the press. (The city of Detroit gets nothing but bad press.) My conversion from Brooklyn Dodgers to Detroit Tigers was facilitated by the ownership treachery of a cross-country flight. Gradually, as I took my son to games or listened to Ernie Harwell on a transistor radio, I found myself loving, not just *baseball* (which is always there) but *a team*: *my* players, *my* team of destiny. During a twi-night double-header with Kansas City, my small son and I watched a skinny right-hander come out of the bullpen, long man in a hopeless cause, and strike out practically everybody, inning after inning: We witnessed the invention of Dennis McLain.

As 1968 began the Tigers seemed to be going nowhere, again—there were extraordinary *holes* in this team, like three-quarters of the infield—but as the season progressed McLain's remarkable pitching combined with strong help from the bullpen, and Gates Brown became the universe's most consistent pinch hitter: The 1968 Tigers won twenty-seven games in their *last* at-bat, and won the pennant pulling away.

But Mayo Smith had problems. Ray Oyler, who was regular shortstop, hit .135 for the season. A more troublesome problem was the status of Al Kaline, who had played twenty years for the Tigers, jumping from his Baltimore high school to the American League in 1953 without ever playing in the minor leagues. He had never played in a World Series, and, as it turned out, 1968 would be his only chance. The aging rightfielder contributed relatively little to the Tigers' great year. He broke his arm in May and a young outfield took over: The Boys from Syracuse, where the Tigers salted and otherwise seasoned their Triple-A players, were Willie Horton in left, Mickey Stanley in center, and Jim Northrup in right. Northrup, who led the team with ninety ribbies, had a penchant for the grand slam; he hit four during the season and one in the Series. Horton hit thirty-six home runs in the season. Stanley hit only .259, but drove in sixty runs; in addition, he played the best defensive centerfield in the major leagues. When Kaline returned from his injury, Smith hesitated to bench a young outfielder; Kaline played some first base while Norm Cash slumped; then Cash started hitting, .333 from July 27th to the end of the season. Kaline became almost a utility man; his hitting suffered, and when he dropped a fly ball at Tiger Stadium in August he heard boos for the first time.

It was unthinkable to bench Al Kaline and his bat for the World Series, but who would sit down? Smith gave thought to substituting Kaline for Don Wert at third base. Wert hit a mere .200—how many teams have won pennants when the left side of the infield combined to hit .175?—but he was a solid defensive player. The Cardinals were *fast*—and if Kaline played third the Cardinals would bunt him into an early grave.

It was the late Norm Cash who suggested that Mayo Smith move Mickey Stanley from centerfield to shortstop. Now Cash and his manager did not get on: First base was an open job as long as Mayo managed, and Cash's opinion of Smith's intelligence was available to any reporter. Yet when Cash spoke his piece about Stanley—"He can play shortstop"—Smith listened. Of course it was general knowledge, as Bill Freehan put it, that Mickey Stanley was "the best all-around athlete we've got."

It takes experience, as well as a talented body, to play shortstop. Only a few coaches, groundskeepers, and Norman Cash knew that Mickey Stanley, all season long, had taken thousands of grounders at shortstop before batting practice. He was twenty-six years old, intense, nervous, and every day the first ballplayer to arrive at the park. When someone showed up who could hit fungos, Stanley worked out taking grounders. He was not auditioning—Mickey Stanley loved centerfield—but burning up excess energy and enjoying himself: He loved to play the game. When Cash strolled out to first base among the earlybirds, he watched Stanley scoop grounders and felt the thrust of Stanley's arm.

During the Tigers' remarkable season, Smith had been forced several times to switch positions. The day after Kaline broke his arm, Bill Freehan ended the game in rightfield. From time to time, first base was occupied not by Cash but by Freehan, Kaline, or Stanley. Midseason the Tigers suffered what someone called "an acute infield shortage." Tommy Matchick owed weekends to the Army Reserve and Dick McAuliffe was suspended for breaking Tommy John in a protest over headhunting. With McAuliffe and Matchick both unavailable for an August doubleheader, Stanley ended the first game coming in from centerfield to play shortstop when Oyler departed for a pinch hitter.

In the second game Stanley started at second base, the fifth Tiger to play the position that season. (Once that summer Mickey Lolich pinch hit; another time Danny McLain was a pinch runner.)

A week before the World Series, Smith made up his mind to play Kaline in his familiar rightfield, bench Oyler, play Northrup in center, and move Stanley from centerfield to shortstop. For practice, Stanley started at shortstop the last six games of the regular season. In his first game at Baltimore he made two errors. But he also made, not a scorekeeper's *error*, but a novice's *mistake*: Throwing to first base to complete a doubleplay, he *stood there* while Don Buford barreled into him. When you take infield before a game, you don't dodge spikes. That night Stanley called Mayo Smith's hotel room. "I asked him if he was sure that this is what he wanted. 'I'm not worried for me; I'm worried for the other players.' He said, 'I know you can do the job; that's good enough for me.' He said, '*You are my shortstop*.'"

Ernie Harwell—who started broadcasting baseball in 1948, and broadcast more than thirty years for the Tigers—always remained astonished by Mayo Smith's decision, because of all the managers Harwell ever described over a microphone, Smith was the most conservative, the most bound by The Book. In baseball's received wisdom, you *Do Not Switch Positions When the Game Is on the Line*. An authoritative spokesman for this opinion is John McGraw, who tells us, "When you shift a man from where he belongs, to strengthen another position, you weaken yourself in both spots." Ray Oyler might hit .135 but he knew what a shortstop knows: to go in the hole; to set himself to throw; when to charge and when to lay back; when to cheat; what bag to cover. Although Northrup was a competent centerfielder, he was no Mickey Stanley in getting to a fly ball or in hitting the cut-off man. When Ernie Harwell before the Series asked opinions from twenty-some old-timers, he found *not one* who approved of Mickey Stanley playing shortstop. Arthur Dailey summed it up in the New York *Times*: Stanley's "credentials must be suspect."

As the Series came closer the buzzing over Smith's decision grew louder. No position-switch so eccentric had ever been tried in a World Series. A manager might realign the order of his pitchers, and Curt Davis start the first game instead of Whitlow Wyatt; or Jim Konstanty might come out of the bullpen to start the Series—but to play an amateur shortstop was another order of the unexpected.

Skeptical press-noises were nothing to the noises inside Mickey Stanley's head; he was not a phlegmatic sort. The night before opening in St. Louis, he borrowed a sleeping pill from his wife; in the morning he popped a tranquilizer; then before the game he vomited anyway. "I suppose," he told Red Smith, "the first damn ball will be hit to me." And it was. He grabbed Lou Brock's grounder and although he looked awkward threw him out with ease. Later he handled doubleplays, tagged base stealers, and took twenty-nine chances to finish the Series with only two errors on balls hit deep in the hole, both errors questionable. In the second game he started a difficult doubleplay in the sixth inning that helped Lolich out of trouble and preserved the Tigers' first win. He batted a mere .214, less than his season's .259 but considerably more than Oyler's .135. In the seven games he made four runs out of two walks and six hits, one a triple. More important, players who might have been sitting performed as they had to: Jim Northrup averaged only .250 but hit two home runs and with eight ribbies tied for the most with Kaline; Kaline hit .379 and Norman Cash .385. Wert hit only .118—but he committed no errors.

It was because of these figures that, when the Tigers won, Norm Cash boasted: "I think the whole damn World Series was Mickey Stanley playing shortstop!"

Mickey Stanley stayed with the Tigers, his only club, until 1978. Since then, he has prospered as a manufacturer's representative to the automotive industry. He could have stayed in baseball; the Tigers offered him a manager's job in Class A, or a job as a major league coach. But he wanted to see more of his children and to make more money. "The day I got my release, I was out pounding on doors. Back in those days we didn't get much money. It has worked out *real* well." Twenty years after his World Series, he seemed as full of nervous energy as he did when he was twenty-six. I arrived at his large and handsome house overlooking Silver Lake in South Lyon (minutes from Ann Arbor, an hour from Detroit) to interview him on a snowy morning in January of 1988 at 7:00 A.M., the earliest interview I have ever done. When I walked toward his door I saw Mickey Stanley through a window: He sat in an easy chair, frown-lines gathered, studying a computer printout.

Stanley had put on ten deeply regretted pounds in the last ten years; the strong lines of his face, lightly sketched in 1968, dug in more deeply as he approached forty-six; and he was as polite as the young man who addressed older reporters as "Sir" back in 1968.

Stanley played basketball and football as well as baseball in his Grand Rapids high school, which he left in 1961 for a Tiger contract, turning down an athletic scholarship to college. He came up to the Tigers briefly at the end of 1964, briefly a year later, and in 1966 stayed up. In high school he had pitched and swung a heavy bat. As a major leaguer his lifetime average was .248; his outfield defense, his versatility, and his amiability kept him on the roster. In his fifteen years wearing a Detroit Tigers uniform, he played 1289 games in the outfield, 94 at first base, 74 at shortstop, 18 at third base, and 4 at second.

He was best in the outfield. He was fast; he studied and cheated and got a good jump; he became a great gymnast or tumbler to catch the ball. Jerry Green, who saw it, describes a famous 1968 catch in Chicago: "Stanley ran sixty yards diagonally across right center and made a diving catch of Tom McGraw's drive. He tumbled onto the gravel track, arose and doubled Louis Aparicio at first base." Whenever he slumped at the plate, as he remembers, his defense improved: "You want to stay in the line-up." He worked endlessly on his hitting, especially with batting coach Wally Moses who believed in him. "Wally Moses got me where I was. He went to bat for me." (I appreciated his metaphor.) In 1968, "he said he would get me to bat .260. I hit .259 and Wally lost a case of Canadian Club."

Although I watched his incredible play in the Series, there

was at least one subtlety of performance that I lacked the know-how to judge. I always wondered about Stanley's range. Although he made only two errors, were there balls he didn't get to, that Oyler might have reached? Mickey Stanley never thought so; in those days he was *fast*—as fast as Oyler, as fast as Trammel in later years—though he hastened to assure me that he *knows* he was no Ozzie Smith. Range was not a problem; what worried him were *situations*: doubleplays; steals; bunts; pick-off plays. "But because I played centerfield, all of that was in front of me all the time." Everything fell into place and he knew what to do: He knew more than he knew he knew. "I went to the right place—because I had seen it happen so many times in front of me." It helped to be surrounded by old hands; Don Wert was at third, and "Dick McAuliffe was second-baseman and he kept me loose. He'd laugh and make a joke of it. Which was relaxing."

Twenty years after the fact Mickey Stanley could not remember his doubleplays, his tags, his throws. I asked, "Can you remember your errors?" He laughed. "I remember them vividly! Both of them were balls hit in the hole. One was way back in the grass. I dove, got the ball, rolled over—I was short leftfield by this time—and then I couldn't find the ball. Javier got to second base." The disinterested Red Smith remained skeptical about the scorer's opinion: "The resident friends who are moonlighting as official scorers charged Stanley with an error on the best play of the Series thus far."

Late in games when the Tigers led, Oyler returned to shortstop, Stanley to center, and Northrup to left while Willie Horton sat down—which improved defense at three positions. But by the end of the Series, no one was worrying about Mickey Stanley at shortstop.

So why not turn full-time shortstop? Next winter, the Tiger management left Ray Oyler unprotected in the expansion draft and the Seattle Pilots took him. Mickey Stanley found himself penciled in as regular shortstop for the Detroit Tigers in 1969. Although he enjoyed centerfield, "I was really looking forward to that: To start a new career, playing shortstop." And there was another reason: "I thought I could make more money: A .250 hitter playing shortstop is more valuable than a .250 hitter playing centerfield."

But he hurt his arm, and a shortstop's arm is even more crucial than a centerfielder's: "I went to spring training. Being young and not *too* intelligent, I . . . Well, the first ground ball of spring training was hit to me in the hole. It was the first fungo that Dick Tracewski hit—not because he *tried* to hit it in the hole; it was *his* first fungo of the spring!—and instead of fielding the ball clean, getting planted, and throwing the ball gently to first, I had to make a foolish low off-balance throw.

"I hurt my arm. My arm was never the same. I didn't play a game all spring training, because of my arm, and when I was opening-day shortstop, I couldn't throw. I spent the rest of my career with a sore arm, with a bad arm. I *really, really* hurt my career with that throw. I don't know how I lasted fifteen years. When I moved back to the outfield—nobody *used* to, ever, run on me—now, sometimes, people took chances. That was embarrassing."

The World Series of 1968, when he played shortstop and

saved the day, was the great moment of Mickey Stanley's base-ball life; and it was virtually the *last* moment, although he played ten posthumous years in the major leagues. Fifty games at shortstop in 1969 showed that he could not do the job. Acquired from the Yankees, Tom Tresh took over at short and Stanley moved back to centerfield. As a centerfielder he tried to fake out the opposition, not to let them recognize how bad his arm was. He also tried to conceal the damage from his own management. "Were they going to release me because I was not throwing at anything close to major league standards? *Constant pressure*. I felt fortunate to play the next years . . . I could still go *catch* the ball! How many guys does a centerfielder throw out? If you use your head and charge the ball, cut down on the distance between outfield and infield, by being aggressive . . .

"*I* knew how different my arm was. Maybe others didn't know. I didn't advertise it. Every day when infield was practicing and outfielders were taking their positions, I would not line up in the normal position, but come in thirty feet . . . I did everything I could to keep people from noticing." I said that it didn't sound like much fun. "It wasn't fun. When all you've done for twenty years is throw, and that's your biggest asset, and you lose that . . . The last years were not good . . . 'When are they going to release me?' "

A manufacturer's representative needs many attributes but not a rifle for a right arm. Mickey Stanley enjoyed his new life and his work. I got the notion—talking baseball on a cold January morning—that he was anxious to get started, to drive to Grand Rapids, talk business, take orders . . .

Talking about the last ten worrisome years of baseball, he entered a blue place in his life. He didn't want to leave me there. As I rose to go, I could feel him searching for something brighter to send me off with. "The thing that really helped me," he supplied, "was that Lou Brock took advantage of the situation. Or *tried* to. There is no doubt in my mind that he was trying to hit the first ball toward shortstop. With a half swing he hit it my way. It had a nice big hop and I threw him out and that took off a *lot* of the pressure." This notion surprised me; I had not considered that Brock hit toward the novice shortstop by design. "How do you know he was doing it on purpose?"

"There is no doubt in my mind. He takes a *good* swing at the ball." Then he corrected his present tense—as we stood in his opulent house, moving toward the door, and 8:00 A.M. dawn turned the snow blue, two decades after a nauseated twenty-six-year-old handled a ground ball—and continued, "He hit home runs. He was just doing a little *punch job* over there. Now, if he had waited for five or six innings, and the bases were loaded, things might have been different . . ."

PITCHING FOREVER

Space, Time, and Baseball
1.

Baseball carries its own time with it, its own motion and stillness; baseball runs counterclockwise.

In *The Natural*—the 1983 Robert Redford movie about a baseball player equally talented and unlucky—the director goes into slow-motion whenever a baseball moment enlarges itself in the direction of Myth. This distortion of clock-time, possibly a touch pretentious, feels almost correct to the imagination seasoned by baseball: Variations on tempo and stasis allow baseball to abandon the everyday streets. Baseball leaves city and suburb behind to engage a strange simultaneousness, a great single continuous day, where—in the words of Meister Eckhart, who was not speaking of baseball—"God cancels the successiveness of men."

In normal American time, sequence is everything: freeway-time, working-day-time, assembly-line-time, television-time. The day flows without pausing, like the second hand on a clock—until, of course, it *stops* with death. Most games and sports occupy this flow-time, with adventitious interruptions for penalties, injuries, and television commercials. The great world-sport of soccer happens in flow-time; basketball happens in flow-time, the one wholly American game. These sports run up and down, and back and forth, but their time drifts like a canal between precise and crafted banks, elapsing steadily with the clock's hand—against the cut-off chopper of the sudden end, whistle or buzzer or gun. They flow against cease. Rugby occupies flow-time, as does American football—which displays the most annoying time-style: several dozen six-second Historical Events situated in an eternity of Standing Around.

Baseball endures periodic interruption, as innings change— but with baseball the interruption is not merely change of direction: It is the monstrous reversal of one against nine, nine against one. The same creatures drop the shield and raise the spear, moving from glove to bat. When places and stances have been reversed, the game re-enters baseball-time, which is a time as unique as the game and its cousins, not to mention its elder brother cricket. Cricket-time is like baseball's, only slowed down. *Slow-down* is a feature of baseball-time. When an American dislikes baseball, it is because the game is slow; when an American loves baseball, it is because the game is slow.

The pitcher controls baseball-time. Certain personalities undertake to become pitchers precisely because they enjoy controlling things. "*Nothing can happen*," I heard an emphatic pitcher boast, "*until I throw that ball*." Of course this defensive leader desires to throw the ball so carefully that "nothing happens" to the dear object.

For those who love baseball, its nothings are something.

Baseball's great single continuous day occupies the moment *before* the ball is pitched. While nothing happens at all, in the static hush between pitches, outfielders stare at the sun's position (truest baseball happens in daytime) and commit it to memory; they arch their necks like horses, pull at their underwear like kindergartners, carefully count men on base, note the number of outs and the ball-strike count. Then these statisticians of vacancy lean forward, hands on their slightly bent knees. The first baseman, if he holds a runner on, leans over with his mitt poised in front of the bag—mitt as gross as a saxophone, mitt as distended as an amaryllis. The second baseman and the shortstop have exchanged confidences (about bases to cover) like middle-school girlfriends planning a telephone call. The third baseman, heroic and solitary, tells his options as a monk tells his beads; or his manager decides for him, and he creeps closer to the bag, preventing an extra-base hit late in the game. At the plate the enemy swings his weapon, Ajax immortal with a club the size of a mammoth tusk: Arms and the man I sing, arms the size of beef-quarters. The catcher flashes fingers-by-numbers with his ungloved hand, dark in the shadow of his crotch, like a mad Calabrian playing Odds-or-Evens solitaire. He points his finger in, out, up, down . . . Meanwhile—this narrative which takes two minutes to read describes 1.5 seconds of clock-time—the pitcher glares in the direction of batter and catcher. Soon, very soon, when the pitcher unwinds himself and lets go, something will happen.

But in baseball-time, we have left the clock behind us. Nothing is over, and nothing is ongoing except everything. By entering baseball-time, we walk into the great day where successiveness is canceled. Now is always; now is forever; now is Wrigley Field and Yankee Stadium. Babe Ruth kneels on deck. Young Walt Whitman saunters at the edge of the outfield grass—lazy, wearing a flower, chewing on a leaf of grass—who will later report this game for the *Brooklyn Eagle*. Batter is Shorty Slagle, who faced Christy Mathewson's fastball at the Polo Grounds seventy years ago; batter is Roberto Clemente, whose generous bones roll in a crashed fuselage under the sea, those are pearls that were his eyes; batter is Wade Boggs, Joe DiMaggio, Henry Aaron, Pie Traynor; pitcher is Walter Johnson, Van Lingle Mungo, Sandy Koufax, Vida Blue; pitcher is also a boy, name unrecorded, who died of influenza in 1919, who would have won more games than Cy Young.

Then the real, temporary pitcher on the only mound of our lives allows time to move again; his own spring uncoils itself, and we enter the brief flow-time of the team sport called baseball. The ball hurtles spinning for sixty feet and six inches—and we *play ball*, again.

After the intense intercourse of pitcher and batter, flow-time alters the number from two to ten in its lighted circle. Ten young knickered players act: Seeing the way the ball moves toward the plate, or having picked up the catcher's sign, infielders and outfielders move, lean, or cheat; maybe the third-baseman and his colleague on first run toward the plate looking for the bunt while the second-baseman covers first base and the shortstop second—leaving great holes for the canny batter to ground singles through . . .

Because . . . the good athlete slows time down. The best hitter on his best day reads the spin of the ball when it leaves the pitcher's hand, and in a nanosecond of baseball-time reflects on his options—reading the ball's motion, reading the infielders' positions—before the ball reaches him. But also the watchers—lovers of baseball, you and I, observers attent and learned—slow time down as the athlete does. We make in our own heads a slow-motion like *The Natural*'s. Abandoning for a while the hectic traffic-time of the contingent day, we enter through baseball an alternative universe where the game's not over until it's over, which is never because it plays itself day and night, winter and summer, where the static is ecstatic and a miraculous sun stands still.

2.

For some of us the game is Fenway Park, with Roger Clemens and Oil Can Boyd; with Billy Bucks, Jim Rice, and perennial failure; with Fenway's classy old-fashioned city-scape, set in the middle of turnpikes and factories, tenements, schools, and shops. Or the game's shape is Dodger Stadium, sculpted out of a stolen ravine under the phlegmy dome of Los Angeles. It is even the dread duplicate shapes, Andy Warhol replicas, of Pittsburgh and Cincinnati. At baseball's heart is a repeated shape; the flattened diamond stays the same forever.

As we fly over southern California we see below us the ten thousand patterns of basepath-and-grass. High over Maine forests, over deserts of Arizona, even over Rocky wastes, we spy

from our cramp and discomfort, elevated to five miles, the small
human landscape and geometry of baseball. Even over Italy and
Japan, even over China, we see beneath us footprints of the
game. World enough we have, from five miles up, as the air-
plane contributes eternity's viewpoint to the human imagination. From our vertical perch we confirm the horizontal game.

As when we see, rising from the flat greenfield of the game,
hovering above the bleachers, the great high-rises of the team's
city. The city brings grass and horizontality into itself by means
of the game, reassuringly touches itself with the earth's honest
flatness staked out against the earth's curve. World enough we
have, but time is another matter, as Einstein said to the actress.
Our time is acceleration, progressive and geometrical. If our
grandfather's diamond is ours, his glove is not nor is his bat. His
glove looks like Mickey Mouse's only skinnier; his bat shows
the marks where he turned it on a lathe. It's true that the swing
remains; we can tell from old images: The line of that swing
connects us by its sibilant swoop, an S of beauty, as leg sweeps
up through trunk to arms extended into bat that exists to extend
arm. This line by necessity runs counter to the pitcher's line
whose front leg rears and plunges, whose rear leg soars, whose
arm rips mightily forward following-through to *put something
on* the whitest ball, or "spheroid" as the poet says. These lines
of force and this forceful rhetoric wind us back, back to our
grandfather's game, back to his grandfather's game who played
outside Shiloh.

We remember, we memorialize, we invent: *forever*, as we
like to think. The daily life—so fragile and frail—we make as

permanent as geometry and bronze; we make a bronze geometry of heroes. When Pausanias, a medical man of the Athenian persuasion who flourished in the second century after Christ, traveled throughout Greece to write about what he saw, he looked far back to heroic times of his city's greatness (Pericles, Thucydides, Plato, Sophocles) six or seven hundred years before his time. He spoke proudly of Greek traces and ruins, as today a European might write about thirteenth-century cathedrals. Pausanias named ten thousand sculptures that no longer exist, gods and heroes; also he commemorated the names of thousands of carved perpetual athletes and copied down ancient poetic inscriptions recounting their triumphs. As Pindar, 500 B.C., wrote odes about wrestlers and runners, so the classic sculptors carved and modeled the likeness of a sixteen-year-old girl who won her race and of a man who won two thousand races and kept running and winning at fifty.

It is by baseball, and not by another American sport, that our memories bronze themselves. Other sports change too fast, rise with the high-rise, mutate for mutability, modify to modernize. By baseball we join hands with the long line of forefathers dead. Thus a player now in his prime looks back fifteen years to when he played semi-pro at thirteen in Mississippi. ("The umpires would have whiskey bottles sticking out of their pockets.") He looks back because baseball occupies historical time, and because Dennis Boyd's father, who ran the Meridian A's, told his son that his grandfather also played here "around the turn of the century," when he wasn't allowed in the white man's leagues. Here Willie Boyd himself pitched to Hank Aaron and Willie

Mays. Here six Boyd brothers of Dennis's generation played together on one team.

Maybe I've seen this familiar diamond from five miles up. Dear flat patch of green and brown. Maybe I see it now, maybe you do too, for it is now and then, the prevailing baseball field. The shape endures and the Can plays the forever game, as he rambles with the shape of it: "I play the game for the love of it, just like my father and my friends, their fathers and their friends. I want to last a long time and pitch grayhaired, like Gaylord Perry and Satchel.

"I'd like to pitch forever, I guess."*

---

*Maybe he will. In 1994 Oil Can Boyd was pitching in a minor league.

GENERATIONS OF
CARLTON FISK

In the summer of 1991 I had breakfast with Carlton Fisk at a Boston hotel on a day when his Chicago White Sox played the hometown team. As I waited by the elevator for the aging all-star—the year he would turn forty-four—I remembered a night sixteen years before. What a game, and what a World Series. October of 1975 was our first October back in New Hampshire, after years of Michigan and the Detroit Tigers. That autumn the maple glories and the glories of oak and aspen flourished my soul. I returned to the childhood paradise of the family farm, and I knew I would never leave it again. To top my ecstasy off, the Red Sox won the pennant and played the Cincinnati Reds for Championship of the Known Universe. In the twelfth inning of the sixth game, Carlton Fisk at twenty-seven hit a home run to win it—using body English to keep it fair, and when the ball hit the screen he leapt, *leapt*, **leapt** along the first base line. The heart of New England leapt with him. Oh, I *grant* we lost the seventh game. We always lose the seventh game.

The elevator door opened and the upright figure of Carlton

Fisk strode forth smiling and holding out a hand. I found it hard to credit his antiquity; he looked like a boy. Heaven knows, in his body Carlton Fisk didn't feel like one: The winter before, to prepare himself for this season, Fisk had undergone operations on both of his knees—not for the first time. As we talked during breakfast he acknowledged: The pain was so great, when he woke every morning, that early in the season he had thought of unbuckling his catcher's carapace forever. It was better, now— but still he woke up feeling as if he had "fallen out of a tree." He continued that summer to play the game; and in July he became the oldest player ever to get a hit in an all-star game.

We talked for two hours about his childhood; about the generations of Fisks in Charlestown, New Hampshire; about his major league decades, about baseball now. Fisk came up to the Red Sox in 1969, which made him a four-decade player in 1990, and he has lived to become an Old Master. In June I watched Chicago's Jack McDowell throw a wild pitch past Fisk with a runner on first. The ball rolled far enough so that the runner could run to second, not far enough for him to make third. With the indolent power of a large cat—a cat who bench-presses more than three hundred pounds—Fisk walked calmly to pick the ball up. He did not waste energy (or hot-dog) by scampering when he did not need to scamper.

On the other hand, watch him sprint out a pop-up. This Leonardo of the diamond crouches on reconstructed knees, night after night, to play the game with sagacity—and with an ethic: Not long ago, Fisk made headlines with his outrage at a rookie on another team who refused to run out a flyball. From behind the plate he snapped, "Run it out, you piece of crud!" After reflection, when the young player came to bat again, Fisk laid down the law the way Moses laid the tablets down: "There is a right way and a wrong way to play this game. You're playing it the wrong way."

For breakfast Fisk ordered no eggs or bacon or ham or steak or pancakes with syrup; he ordered 1990: oatmeal, English muffins, juice, and coffee. Chatting, he was humorous, pleasant, and articulate. His frankness revealed itself when I mentioned a star of the game. "He's dumb as a stick," said Fisk. I must have looked shocked—surprised not by the allegation but by the candor—for he felt driven to qualify: "Well, *I* think he's dumb as a stick." As breakfast continued I observed Fisk's gentlemanliness, as well as his wit and intelligence. Oatmeal finished and juice glass empty, we'd both run out of coffee. Carlton Fisk addressed the waitress: "Can we have some more coffee, when you're done?" (There is a right way and a wrong way to address a waitress.) Of all the athletes that I've talked with in twenty years of writing about sports, this is the man I like best.

We talked about his childhood in New Hampshire. Carlton Fisk's parents ran a tight ship. There were six children to feed and clothe on wages from the Jones and Lamson Machine Company. Each child had duties to perform—garden to weed, yard to maintain, manure to spread in spring, snow to shovel in winter. Fisk told me a story from his eighth year, when he came to supper without having finished his chores—the night his favorite *Zorro* showed on TV. Like many American families, the Fisks had a TV; but in Charlestown privilege was conditional upon work. Telling the story, Fisk mimicked his father Cecil's stentorian voice: "Then—There—Will—Be—No—TV—To-night." Carlton burst into tears and hurtled from the table to finish his tasks outdoors in the dark; his program finished before he did.

Thirty-six years after missing *Zorro*, he makes his point: His life as a child was demanding but it was disciplined, consistent, and fair. Carlton Fisk understands: His background made his foreground; his childhood created his manhood.

The Fisk household entertained no suburban notions of allowances for children, and Carlton earned his pocket money by delivering papers, mowing lawns, shoveling snow from roofs, and weeding gardens for arthritic elders. When he was old enough, he worked summers laying pipe for the water and sewer department of the town, and—the hardest job—poured concrete for a contractor, working in good weather from 5:00 A.M. to sundown.

There were diversions. Charlestown High played only three sports: Carlton Fisk excelled at soccer, basketball, and baseball. Basketball was his favorite, and he centered a team that won a state title in 1963. (In one tournament game, he scored forty points and took down thirty-six rebounds.) Baseball occupied his summers when he was not laying pipe or pouring concrete. He played shortstop, pitched, and caught in Babe Ruth and American Legion ball for Claremont and for Bellows Falls in Vermont across the Connecticut River. For one year after high school, he led the University of New Hampshire freshman basketball team. Then after a stint in the Army, he signed a Red Sox contract: no more basketball.

Twenty-five years later, he works out all winter, hours every day. Relentlessly his body seeks the condition of youth, and he is still quick on his feet, but he is also middle-aged. During breakfast he talked like most of us who, growing older, regret the past. "I've seen the players and their attitudes regress," he said. "The older players used *the game* as the only motivating factor." He grimaced. "Now it's the dollar sign. They want to be paid but they don't want to pay the price." Fisk enjoys his wages, but he means to earn them. Maybe as he spoke he realized that he gave too puritanical an impression, for he went on to remember youthful major league antics unmodified by a work ethic: "We used to sit around, drinking, until three or four in the morning—but we were talking *ball*. The biggest thing missing now is camaraderie."

Today, Carlton Fisk plays with athletes he could be father to. It must be intimidating for young players to talk *ball* with a man who caught in the bigs before they were born.

From growing up with his grandfather and father in Charlestown, Fisk remembers models of male aging. Soberly he remembered his father as rigorous ship's captain; smiling he remembered his father as middle-aged athlete. "We'd go over to the barn and shoot baskets." This was his grandfather's barn, nearby, where he and his brothers shot at a hoop nailed to a hayloft beam over the barn floor. "One time, we were practicing shooting foul shots while my father was milking the cow. Somebody made ten or fifteen. My father came into the barn wearing his barn coat and his barn boots, took his coat off, kept his boots on, and shot thirty-eight in a row." He grinned, shaking his head.

It is ironic and a source of regional distress that this pure product of New Hampshire may wear a White Sox cap on his Cooperstown plaque. He caught nine productive years for the Red Sox, but in 1981 the Red Sox failed to meet a contract deadline—accidentally on purpose; bad blood between Fisk and a boss, which probably cost the Red Sox the 1986 World Series—and New Hampshire's Carlton Fisk slipped away to play out his long athletic life in the Midwest.

Maybe when baseball is over, the Fisks will return to their New England, and the generations will continue in the Connecticut valley. Or maybe Carlton and Linda will remain in Illinois, where their children have grown up. They vacillate on the subject. As he mulled it over, Carlton recalled how his father bought a cow when milk prices went up early in the 1950s. Care of the cow became routine for the Fisk children, and for three weeks in August (vacation from the mill) this family hayed and filled the barn together—instead of basking on Cape Cod or camping in the mountains. Naturally, the Fisk family also raised a large vegetable garden, upwards of an acre, and Leona Fisk directed a summer of canning—hundreds of quarts of peas, beans, corn, carrots, and beets. Like their neighbors, the Fisks left parsnips in the ground all winter to eat fresh when frost left the ground. Fisk complains that he cannot find a parsnip *anywhere* around Chicago. Maybe parsnips will bring him home.

THAT SWING IN 1941

The summer of 1941 I was twelve and began to hay with my grandfather Wesley at Eagle Pond Farm. My first hay day, I learned how to pull a bullrake and clean up the hayfield after my grandfather pitched on. We talked that summer about the war in Europe and when—not if—the United States would belong to it. Almost alone among New Hampshire farmers, my grandfather was a New Deal Democrat—in favor of F.D.R., of Lend Lease, of anything that opposed "old Hitler." Of course we also talked about times gone by, as we always did; he loved to tell stories as much as I loved to hear them. And that summer we talked about Ted Williams and whether he might hit .400.

It was a great baseball summer, goodness knows—the last great one for a while. We were aware of goings-on at Yankee Stadium where a DiMaggio—the wrong flavor of DiMaggio; Joe's brother Dom played for the Red Sox—hit safely for fifty-six straight games. I was a Brooklyn Dodger fan, which meant that I cherished as deep an antipathy toward the Yankees as my grandfather did—who had rooted for Boston's American

League team since 1902, when Cy Young won thirty-three games. Nobody batted .400 in 1902, but it happened often during my grandfather's baseball lifetime. Ty Cobb did it twice, .420 in 1911 and .410 in 1912. Nobody had managed .400 for seventeen years (since Rogers Hornsby, .424 in 1924) but now, the last prewar summer, it looked as if a leftfielder with a classic natural swing—twenty-three years old that season—might reach .400 again.

We had an arrangement, my grandfather and I, whereby he rooted for the Dodgers in the National League and I for the Red Sox in the American. By necessity in 1941 we were newspaper fans. The Red Sox were on the radio, but we couldn't listen; games were still afternoon affairs at Fenway Park—no lights until 1947—and they played while we hayed. If it rained in New Hampshire so we didn't hay, it rained in Boston so they didn't play. We rested on the Sabbath—and in my grandmother's sabbatarian parish, the radio rested also.

Our season arrived every day at noontime—one day late—when we picked up the Boston *Post* which arrived by mail a mile down the road at Henry Powers's post office and store. Every day we checked out Boston and Brooklyn. In the American League the Yankees looked unbeatable, but in the National League my team was thriving. With Peewee Reese, Pete Reiser, Dixie Walker, Joe Medwick, and Micky Owen in the field; with the pitching of Whitlow Wyatt, Kirby Higbee, and Curt Davis—relieved by Hugh Casey—Brooklyn was *en route* to its first pennant in twenty-one years.

But if Boston would win no pennant, at least Ted Williams

continued on a tear, day by day as the summer wore on—almost a hit every other at bat. We looked to the sports pages first thing when we opened the paper. "How did Brooklyn do?" "How many hits did Teddy get?" July fifth he dropped to .400 flat—but by August he had raised it back up to .412. I remember the drawings on the sports pages—Ted driving a run, Ted hitting a homer, Ted with that fabulous, sweet, natural-looking swing.

It wasn't until I was at boarding school three years later that I heard the Duke Ellington song, "It don't mean a thing if it ain't got that swing"—but when I heard it I thought of Ted Williams. Granted that the lyrics do not refer to hitting a baseball, as the song alludes to American swing music—also compact of grace, fluid energy, and completion—it gives me the analogy I want. Duke Ellington's swing, like Ted Williams's, gathered genius, labor, power, practice, concentration, and wit together into one artifact. Yet to the observer, both swings seemed as natural as leaves to the tree. In the history of baseball, no other player's swing seems so natural, so well disguised as a product of talent's abundance.

When memory plays images of that Williams swing, we catch him in stillness, wound on the invisible axis of his balance, turned on himself like a barber's pole in its shapely curving. As the mind's carousel switches from one image to another, from the *Post* to *Sports Illustrated*, the gallery of spirals becomes a helix doubled and tripled by repetition. If we flip these pictures fast enough, they become one sleek mighty ripple through an unlucky pitcher's pitch—starting from the attent sleek cat-coil of waiting, releasing in a surge of pivoting hips to extend powerful arms, concluding with the satisfying *re*coil of the follow-through. There's motion implicit in every millimeter of arrest, always turning on itself, powerfully contained within its cylinder.

In his book, *The Science of Hitting*, Ted Williams makes the observation—with Heraclitus, Longinus, and Freud—that we progress by the reconciliation of opposites, dialectics or irony here applied to hitting a baseball: "It's a pendulum action. A metronome—move and countermove . . . you throw a ball that way, you swing a golf club that way, you cast a fishing rod that way." Always thesis and antithesis roll into synthesis. You hit that way, as you write a poem or drive a car or run a business that way: *move and countermove*. You play a piano that way.

When the 1941 season ended, I was back in Connecticut at Spring Glen Grammar School, relishing the Dodgers' National League pennant—and looking forward to next summer at Eagle Pond. My grandfather wrote one of his rare letters, carved in pencil, congratulating me on the Dodgers (we lost the World Series to the Yankees, four games to one) and exulting in the batting average of our Ted Williams: not only the average itself, but how he accomplished it at the end.

When you practice a skill continually, in solitude or in public, it's available when you need it most. That swing was available on the last day of the 1941 season, when Williams had the option of sitting out a doubleheader and ending his great year at .3996, which would have averaged out. Nothing he ever did fitted him so well as his resolution to play, to risk losing the mark. Ted went six for eight that day—as my grandfather marveled, in his pencil'd letter, and as he remembered until he died—and ended his great season at .406.

Next summer we talked not about baseball but war. We continued to remember the great baseball summer of 1941—it sustained us through war-years of mediocre baseball—and what Ted Williams accomplished before going off to the Marines. Later, after the war, I would visit Fenway Park many times while I was at college—and once my father drove my grandfather and me to Fenway for a game, to watch Ted lord it over the batter's box. Our old baseball haying-talk took shape—older, a little thicker—in left field before our eyes.

THE CONTINUOUS PARTY

We moved back to Eagle Pond in the era of Thornley's Store. When you live in the country, stores are crucial enough to give their names to eras. Before Thornley was Don Sturgis, who expanded from an Esso station to an Esso station that sold milk. From that gesture to a proper general store is only a series of small expansions—season after season and owner to owner. Our first winter here I bought the felt-lined boots at Thornley's that I still wear eighteen Februaries later. Also, during that first year, we bought cheese, gas, ketchup, stove pipe, hot dogs, apples, a chainsaw, yogurt, ice cream, nails, soda pop, salt, sugar, crockery bowls, a dozen gifts with Old Man decals, the Boston *Globe*, turnips, paperback novels, ballpoint pens, eggs, hammers, chocolate-covered cherries, wrenches, seeds, doughnuts, and snowshoes.

Only about four hundred yards away, uphill and around a corner where we couldn't see it, Thornley's Store was our landmark when we gave directions: "Next house on the right, after the store." Every day I hit Thornley's at 5:00 A.M., to get the *Globe*, when not even Thornley's was open. Slugabed Bob didn't open until six, or so his sign claimed; like everyone else in New Hampshire, he was always early. If I overslept and didn't pop down for the paper until five-forty-five, Bob noted my tardiness. "Must have been some party last night."

At five I took my paper from the pile which the truck tossed off between gas pumps, cutting the plastic strap with my Barlow knife. On most days we visited Thornley's once or twice; any excuse would do. Jane and I spend many hours sedentary and silent, making illegible marks on paper at our desks. We cherish reasons to stand and move around—like carrying logs from woodshed to woodstove, or like an errand to the store. "Looks like we're low on skim. I'll get it." "No! I'll get it!"

But our pleasure in visiting Thornley's wasn't only the desire to take a break. It was Jane who came up with the right description: Thornley's Store, she said, was a continuous party. Now this party did not resemble the weekend booze-outs in the prosperous town we left when we moved to Eagle Pond, with everybody dressed up, flirting and showing off, eating sausages in puff pastry. This party was more like *carnaval*—Italy or New Orleans or Spain—with each participant costumed in his or her own character on the quick affable stage of Thornley's Store, dropping a one-liner before returning to the car (the key in it, the motor running) and the day's working life.

When we walked through the door, we saw Bob Thornley first—standing behind the counter, smiling and expectant, gregarious and ironic, leaning forward on strong arms with his sleeves rolled up to the elbows. It's hard to believe that Bob is dead; his vitality seemed as natural and as permanent as winter and summer. Last winter, retired to Florida, Bob died after multiple illnesses. Transfusions kept him alive toward the end, but he knew they would not make him well; he declined further blood, saying that somebody else could make better use of it. Then he argued with Ardalee, his soon-to-be widow, over the best restaurant for the gathering after the funeral.

Sometimes Ardalee stood at the counter but more often it was Bob. With many customers he performed a running gag, a tease-of-the-decade that required ritual allusion before other business could be transacted. Subject matter could verge on the dangerous, but the ample benignity of the teaser mixed a *sauce piquante* that never poisoned anybody. If you were a beer drinker or a vegetarian, you might hear about your predilections. If you had recently bent a fender, you might hear mention of your driving skill. When you returned from a vacation, you were sure to hear about your lifestyle of the rich and famous . . . And of course when something miserable happened, you found Thornley sympathy as large and whole as any teasing.

In the store, at any moment, there was always a chorus of the village elders, or juniors, or women young and old. Thornley's Store was an exchange, as you traded in your story or your joke and took away more than you brought. Thornley's Store was where you caught up. If in the night you heard the fire alarm, at Thornley's you found out what burned. After a neighbor's operation, if you were anxious, you didn't need to call the hospital.

Thornley's was a party continually warm, gregarious, and energizing. It was message center and joke mart; it was where you found if someone needed help; it was also the place for solving problems. Did you want somebody to stack wood when your back was out? Did you need a babysitter, with your niece coming? Twenty years ago I arrived in town in need of typing help. Bob thought of Lois—who made these words legible, as she has done since 1975.

It is exhausting to host a party seven days a week for a decade. When the Thornleys sold up, the whole countryside mourned. On the last day we did the right thing, at Jane's instigation: We had a party. Six years later, we did the same for the couple who followed, Marge and Bernie Cornell—who ran a different party which was also the same. This time it was the woman who led the way, whose wit and manic energy kept the institution not only alive but lively, the party ongoing. The Cornells were younger than the Thornleys. When they raised a tall sign, *Cornell's Country Corners*, they looked settled in, and we hoped we might keep them forever. Some of us complained to Marge that we spent all weekend looking for that damned *corner* but we couldn't find one between Concord and Quebec. Marge claimed they'd ordered one out of the Sears catalog.

Keeping a store is too much for practically anybody. Marge and Bernie sold out to the Taylors, who continued to let me pick up the paper at 5:00 A.M.; then, one morning in July, I drove for the *Globe* through the hot rising dew—to find our store burned down to the ground. I gaped at the still smoldering aisles of canned goods, black but recognizable beside exploded wine bottles near the blackened twisted cash register. I gazed incredulous at the whole wide wooden homemade accumulation of hands and decades, collapsed on itself in devastation.

For a week a bulldozer cleaned debris, then dug a hole and buried the charcoal of our store. We heard that the insurance money would not provide for rebuilding. Or maybe the Taylors were discouraged, for they sold their house and barn as quickly as they could and moved away. The store was gone—but the countryside needs a store, so two miles away Billy Sanborn added onto his Junction Gulf garage, and then added more, making the Kearsarge Mini-Mart where I get the *Globe* now at five in the morning. Judy the manager operates the new message exchange and joke mart, crowded with coffee-drinkers at 6:00 A.M. But Mini-Marts don't sell stovepipe.

Downstreet a new family lives in the old house beside the cement foundation that used to be Thornley's—and Sturgis's and Cornell's Country Corners. Sometimes as I drive past the old place I fancy that I still smell creosote. In my mind's eye, I can see the volunteer firemen the day the store burned down: They worked all night to save the house and barn, young men from Wilmot, Danbury, and Andover. Exhausted after hours fighting the fire, they stood watching the last embers flash and smoke as they drank coffee and ate doughnuts provided by the women's auxiliary—these young men tired, grinning, cheerful, telling jokes: seeing the party out to its last end.

GRANDFATHERING

The older I get, the more clearly I recollect a morning when I was a child of eight or nine and attended an auction on the side of Ragged Mountain. Maybe *clearly* is the wrong word, because I know how memories can distort what really happened, in the service of later ideas and experiences. As I tell this story, I must change names and alter circumstances a little. Do I alter other circumstances, without knowing that I do? Probably. If I don't remember the auction clearly, I remember it with strong feeling—and with irony.

The Dobbins Place had been sold, and old Victor was clearing out his family's generations of accumulation. He couldn't take care of the big house any more; I doubt he could pay town taxes. Like many cashless farmers, Victor Dobbins used to work the roads to pay his taxes, but now he was too old to haul hardpan for New Canada Road. (I remember a large white moustache, yellowish over the mouth, a blue cloth cap, faded blue overalls, and a body that moved slowly, dragging the weight of its pain.) Because Victor had no place to go, when he sold the old farm, my grandfather gave him a morsel of pasture land across New Canada Road, where the old man could raise a small camp, with the help of our cousin Freeman who could build anything if he had time enough. The land my grandfather gave Victor was only a third of an acre, shaped like a bite in a slice of bread, and he owned many acres of pasture and wood-lot—but it touches me to remember that my grandfather gave the land away. He had no money but he thought nothing of giving away a houselot; of course the cash value of the land was virtually nothing at the time. By auction-time, I suppose that Victor had moved a few chairs and tables and beds into his camp, skillets and forks and woodstoves and icebox. Everything else was to go. The old place was crowded with *stuff*—like any house where five or six generations, following each other, have never thrown anything away. For the auction, the inside accumulation traveled outside, some things piled on tables, others leaning against weathered clapboard from which the paint had largely fallen away. Indoor possessions like quilts and chamberpots looked alien in the open air, as if they blinked and squinted in sunlight. At first, the mere spectacle took my eyes, as the social occasion took my attention. Peddlers set barrows at the crowd's edge, one with yardgoods and another with cutlery. A tinker strung pots and pans on a rope stretched between an ash and a maple. Freeman had brought his pack, from which to sell Quaker Oil or Rawleigh's Salve if anybody required medical supplies.

People came from a distance. Neighbors and strangers prowled among the goods stacked by the house, fingering and raising to the light. I overheard conversations that exchanged information about kin and old schoolfriends. My grandfather and grandmother greeted old friends as they did on Old Home Day; I was introduced a hundred times as Lucy's boy and, yes, it don't seem possible . . . Bored, I wandered off to visit Riley, tied to a maple at the edge of a hayfield among other horses and buggies. Black Model A's, with an occasional blue Buick, occupied the Dobbins's yard and the ditches of New Canada Road. I found no nine-year-olds to play with—just a few shy small children holding close to skirts and overalls. I wandered gazing at the furniture gathered in the daylight air: four mirrors, two beds, stiff upright dining room chairs, a kitchen table painted farmhouse green, wardrobes, dressers, chests, a Morris chair . . . I examined stacks of bedding, boxes of papers and photographs. Another corner of the yard was heaped with pitchforks and scythes, a bullrake with missing teeth, harness, axes, sapbuckets, saws, ice-saws, milkpails, and milkcans. My grandfather had said something about maybe picking up a good scythe.

Dimly I think I understood, right away, that I was watching the end of something old, the emptying out of something that had been full. As a child in New Hampshire I was witness to many conclusions, and eventually learned the history of this vanishing: Once, somebody had cleared this land—oak by oak, boulder by boulder; maybe the first Dobbins of New Canada Road was a soldier who mustered out of General Washington's Army and trudged north to cut his own land from the woods of a stony hill; or maybe the farm went back further (but not before the English defeated the French in the 1760s, ending the French and Indian Wars) and the original Dobbins lugged his musket from this farm to join General Stark and fight Burgoyne at Bennington . . .

Once Ragged Mountain was dense with farms and farmers—the land clearer in 1790 than it was in 1935. The settlers were people with land, and without cash, who never considered that they lacked anything at all. They had wood for winter and ice for summer, forage for ox and moolycow, chickens for eggs or for plucking and boiling on Sunday, a pig for salt pork and bacon, a vegetable garden for storing and canning, maple trees for one sweet and honeybees for another . . . If we refer to their enterprise as "subsistence farming," the adjective reveals our grudgingness not theirs. For them one notion shone as bright as the king's gold in his coat-of-arms: *The land was their own land*.

Later the turnpike, the canal, industry along the rivers, and especially the railroad turned our economy (and our culture) toward cash. It was a long story, which took many years to conclude. After the middle of the nineteenth century, these hill farms began to extinguish—like the dying whippoorwill now, or like houselights that go out, one by one, across a night valley. Beyond the Dobbins's, the Trumps had abandoned their farm in 1917 and their place collapsed into its cellarhole before I was born. A mile up New Canada, Jim Blasington still worked his farm; two miles further Freeman grew his own food and worked on the road for taxes. My grandfather sold milk, wool, eggs, timber—and got by.

That day at the Dobbins auction I watched the clearing-out of yet another old place that had carried many generations on its stony back. Four years later the Blasington's place burned down and Jim moved in with his brother Cedric. Five years later still, Freeman died, and in a decade his stout camp crumbled.

This Dobbins house would not fall down. Somebody from Toledo had bought it for a summer place. For the next ten or twelve years, my grandfather and I would hay these fields each summer, keeping the acreage tidy for the Ohio people, helping to feed my grandfather's Holsteins so that he could sell blue milk to H. P. Hood & Sons in Boston.

Now the auctioneer held up farm implements for bidding on. My grandfather bought a scythe with a sound snath and an almost-new blade for seventy-five cents. The buggy went—the animals must have gone earlier—and then the kitchen things: My grandmother bought two dozen Ball jars for a quarter. (A dollar was a lot to spend.) When bales of clothes began to go, I started to wake up. I had started with a dim sense of conclusion; now I understood what was concluded. This waking is what I remember—my eight-year-old vision of time and devastation. There were tophats, women's hats with veils, out-of-style overcoats, housedresses, fancy aprons, skirts, gloves still in their Sears boxes, and handkerchiefs. There were albums of photographs and postcard albums; certificates of marriage, baptism, and death; temperance pledges; diaries; and box after box of letters. These boxes—waking, I understood—were stuffed with the lives of dead farmers and farmwives. These lives went for a nickel each, going going gone, as the auctioneer from Bristol dispersed the accumulation of six generations.

The auctioneer's voice chanted rhythms of loss on the summer air. When I went home I wept for the Dobbinses—and I wept for you and for me. Upstairs in our back chamber were broken chairs, chests full of dead people's clothing, captain's chairs, boxes containing pretty Christmas cards, snapshots of kittens and cousins, wads of old letters tied together with brittle twine.

The people from Toledo, who bought the place, got their eggs from my grandmother: "nice folks," they were. When *they* died, as people tend to do, the new people added an enormous heated indoor swimming pool to the old Cape. The pool reached into the field where we hayed, and beyond it the same owners added two tennis courts paved with a green composite. No more haying there—but a little later, my grandfather took his own turn dying. What remained of the hayfield was mowed by one of the new people's handymen sitting on a tractor that pulled six lawnmowers behind it. When Victor Dobbins died, the new people bought his camp to protect themselves. Because Freeman had shingled the roof, the shack stayed upright though the windows broke and the inside filled with leaves. When the new people died, six hundred acres went on the market, all woodlot now, and recently a developer approached the town planning board for a permit to build seventy houses.

Permit not granted. Not yet.

Now in my sixties, and a grandfather myself, I walk with Gus up dirt New Canada Road past Victor's still-standing camp and past the old Dobbins Place concealed under a complex of improvements. Not long ago a real estate agent telephoned to offer

me the third of an acre my grandfather had given to Victor. He
offered me the land as a courtesy, he said, because it nipped into
my woodlot. I don't tell this story against real estate agents or
anybody else; I tell it against the memory of an auction I attended fifty-odd years ago, against history and waking to loss.
The agent suggested that twenty-five-thousand dollars would be
a fair price because the old shack would allow the purchaser to
raise a building without a new permit; the new building would
be grandfather'd, he told me.

WAR CARDS, PURPOSE, AND BLAME

My father was too young for the Great War, not fifteen when it ended, and both of my grandfathers were too old. Their fathers fought in the Civil War—archaic blue figures stiff-bearded in photographs—but in 1937, when I was eight, Gettysburg might have been Agincourt or Marathon. As the new war came closer, I understood that my father felt guilty about missing the Great War, but I understood that he wanted to miss the new one as well. Everyone was nervous, the Depression hanging on and war approaching. I was an only child, alert to my parents' anxiety. My mother was thin and attentive. She came to Connecticut from a remote farm in New Hampshire; and as I grew up, I became aware that she felt lonely in the suburbs. She paid more attention to her child, in her displacement, than she would have done if she had stayed up north with her sisters.

Sometimes she took me on excursions to New Haven—Saturdays during the schoolyear, weekdays in summer. We walked up Ardmore Street to Whitney Avenue and waited for the bus that came every ten minutes to roll us four miles down Whitney and drop us at Church and Chapel outside Liggett's across from New Haven's Green. While I tagged along, she shopped at Shartenberg's and Malley's. When we had done shopping we ate lunch at a place where I ordered beans and franks—two grilled hotdogs and a tiny crock of pea-beans dark with molasses; dessert was jello with real whipped cream or dry yellow cake with white frosting; lunch cost thirty-nine cents.

Then we went to the movies. We saw a first-run film, a B-movie, one or two shorts, previews of coming attractions, and a newsreel. I remember for certain only one film that I saw in 1937, but I'm almost sure that I watched Spencer Tracy in *Captains Courageous*; maybe Paul Muni in *The Life of Emile Zola* and *The Good Earth*; probably *Lost Horizon* and *A Star Is Born*, maybe *One Hundred Men and a Girl*. The only movie I remember for certain, after fifty-some years, is *The Last Train from Madrid*. After we took the bus home to Ardmore Street, I stopped playing at war with my friends.

In 1937 we boys wore long woolen stockings that tucked over the bottoms of corduroy knickers as we walked to Spring Glen Grammar School. There were no schoolbuses. Children from my neighborhood took several different routes to school—for variety, or to avoid a bully or an old best friend who had become an enemy—but we always passed the Glendower Drug Store because it was only two short blocks from school. If we had change in our pockets, we spent it there. For a nickel, we bought big candybars. For one penny, we bought flat pieces of gum creased into five sticks, pink as a dog's tongue, that came with cards illustrating our different obsessions: Of course there were baseball cards, and I seem to remember cards for football as well; I remember G-Man cards, each of which illustrated a triumph of law and order as J. Edgar Hoover's agents flushed out Dillinger—shooting him in the alley outside a movie theatre—or Pretty Boy Floyd. Although G-Man cards were violent, they resembled the Society of Friends alongside another series that we bought and collected. We called them War Cards, and they thrived in the bellicose air of 1937.

For then the war in Spain shrieked from the front pages of newspapers along with the Japanese invasion of China. In 1937 Stalin kept discovering to his astonishment that old colleagues had betrayed him; he shot seven of his best generals that year, doubtless a great advantage when Hitler invaded. In 1937 Trotsky found his way to Mexico, Amelia Earhart disappeared into the Pacific, the UAW invented the sit-down strike, Neville Chamberlain asked Hitler's cooperation in the interest of peace, the *Hindenburg* exploded and burned in New Jersey, Pierce-Arrow shut down, George Gershwin died, Orson Welles and Joseph Cotten appeared on Broadway in *Julius Caesar*, and thousands of American progressives joined the Lincoln Brigade to fight Fascism in Spain. Half of them never returned.

Even in the fourth grade we knew about Hitler, whose troops and planes fought with Franco against the Loyalists, aided by Stalin's troops and planes. Germany was the continuous enemy, less than twenty years after the Armistice of 1918. We were good, brave, loyal, outnumbered, and victorious against all odds; they were evil, cruel, cowardly, vicious, dumb, shrewd, and doomed. *We knew who was right and who was wrong.* (My father's mother's family had emigrated from Germany to New Haven in the last century, which was confusing.) In 1937 all of us—parents, teachers, even children—understood that there would be another war and that America would join it sooner this time. Isolationists and pacificists campaigned against war, but everyone knew that war was inevitable—whether it was or wasn't. A phenomenon like War Cards, as I remember them, makes it seem as if we were being prepared; as if *they* made sure that we grew up expecting to become soldiers, accepting the guns and the bombing.

At least no one—so soon after the Great War—had the temerity to present war as a Cub Scout expedition. When we went to the movies, we saw a newsreel and sometimes even the March of Time. The late 1930s was endless parades in black and white, soldiers marching, weapons rolling past reviewing stands; I remember refugees panicked on the narrow roads, all their possessions piled on donkeys, ancient trucks, or small bent backs. I remember the bombing and strafing of refugees. Ominous deep voices doom-spoke while the screen showed airplanes in formation, or artillery pieces recoiling with little puffs emerging from muzzles like speech-balloons in comic strips. I remember Hitler addressing rallies, immense crowds of identical figures sieg-heiling—robots of outrage and blood that jerked with a single will.

War Cards used a lot of red ink. On the back a short text described a notorious occasion and on the front an artist illustrated what happened. I remember one card which showed a Japanese bomb hitting a crowded Chinese bus, maybe in Shanghai: Bodies coming apart hurtled through the air, intestines stretching between the separated parts of a human figure, headless bodies littering the ground. I don't believe that these cards were clearly ideological; in the United States, there were two ideas about war in Europe—get in or stay out—and these cards seemed neither isolationist or interventionist. (As I recollect the cards carried a line that claimed them to be educational, because they illustrated the Horrors of War.) Of course, it occurred to me later, there wouldn't be much blood for us if we stayed out. Blood was the whole matter; blood was the food on which our boyish deathlove fed itself.

We loved our War Cards, chewing gum as we walked home to add a new one to our collections. If it was a duplicate we could swap, maybe the exploded bus for a card that showed the shelling of a boat. We collected War Cards as we collected ourselves for war. I loved airplanes in 1937 and read pulp stories about dogfights over the trenches. I loved the pilot-heroes of the 1930s—Wiley Post, Amelia Earhart, later Wrong-Way Corrigan. When I imagined myself going to war I joined the Lafayette Espadrille, flew Spads, and shot down Fokker Triplanes. I remember visiting the New Haven airport—later, it must have been—and seeing camouflaged fighter planes and bombers, including the mighty B-17 or Flying Fortress, which in retrospect resembles an ultralight. I remember watching parades on Memorial Day or the Fourth of July: tiny tanks clanking, soldiers marching with Springfield rifles and wearing Great War helmets.

Then I saw *The Last Train from Madrid*. Did it really change my life? The phrase sounds exaggerated, melodramatic. I never registered as a CO. (Nor did I serve in the military.) Although I worked in Ann Arbor with the movement against the Vietnam War, I was never a leader; neither did I spell the country Amerika. It was war-horror that filled my chest, not political commitment: A horror is not an idea, as a shudder is not a conviction. My horror, I think, started with this film. Certain scenes of war retain the power to burst me into tears, especially the random slaughter of civilians. It is hard now to remember the outrage people felt over Guernica—after the bombings of London, Dresden, and Hiroshima—but Picasso's painting registers the shock and incredulity of 1937. I remember, in late adolescence after the war, trying to read an essay that told how French mothers struggled, dreading air raids in 1939, to fix their gas masks onto the tiny heads of their babies. I couldn't finish the page.

In September of 1990 I saw *The Last Train from Madrid* again, fifty-three years after I watched it as an eight-year-old in the Paramount Theater in New Haven. Over the years, I had thought of the film often, and assumed that it was anti-Fascist or Popular Front. It is no such thing; the film that I watched in 1990 is astonishingly without political ideology: Its single import is the randomness of war-horror. Cliches and stereotypes provide a plot, impossible to take seriously. As contemporary reviewers mentioned, the film is derivative—"Grand Hotel" on wheels—and its romantic framework hurries into irrelevance, leaving behind an expressive, almost expressionist, music of nightmare. I do not mean to say that *The Last Train from Madrid* is a good film; it is bad, bad art: The plot is improbable and the motivation incredible; the writing is ghastly, from clumsy exposition to the flattest cliches of dialogue. Yet it terrified me once; it retained much terror fifty-three years later.

The film begins with loud scare sounds and the hurtling image of a locomotive and train. A radio newscast tells us that tonight the last train will leave Madrid, after which—we understand—the city will be overrun by the nameless army that besieges it. The army lacks not only name but idea, and its only purpose is killing. As characters speak of the train's terminus in Valencia, on the other hand, Valencia becomes pure symbol: The destination is Arcadian peace in a countryside antithetic to the city of panic, chaos, and violent death. Naturally, everyone wants a seat on the train. The plot of the movie turns on separate and intermingled stories of people seeking passage on the train—their stratagems, their failures and successes. At the end the train steams out of Madrid carrying some of our people and leaving others behind—not only behind but dead; in the film's emotional terms, *behind* means *dead*.

As the film begins, a noble young officer (noble because he is handsome and stands straight; noble because he is Anthony Quinn) listens to impassioned pleas for passes and in his dutiful nobility refuses them. We dwell on an old lady, well-played, who begs and is refused. Most of our central figures are couples, two-by-two like the ark's animals: the romantic interest, which I doubtless ignored in 1937. It remains easy to ignore in 1990: None of it feels authentic, only partly because Dorothy Lamour (beloved of two leading men) plays her part with the expressiveness of a Malley's manikin. Lew Ayres is in love with

Olympe Bradna, Robert Cummings with Helen Mack—and none of it matters. There is no genuine feeling between men and women. Love between two men matters more—Anthony Quinn and Gilbert Roland—who swore blood brotherhood as soldiers in Africa years before. This male loyalty is stereotypical—*Beau Geste* stuff—but it provides the strongest human bond in the film, its power only less than the forces of panic and dread. Quinn will betray any government or any commanding officer to remain loyal to his blood brother. In all of *Last Train*, we find no economic or political or social ideology; instead, we find the exaltation of private affection and a dream of pastoral peace in the midst of history's nightmare. Doubtless such dreams are conservative; they are not Fascist.

A slaphappy American journalist (Lew Ayres) picks up a girl (Olympe Bradna) who wants to get to Madrid to see her father before the firing squad executes him. (Naturally they fall in love; this pair makes it to the train.) She sees her father, he is executed—and we never receive an inkling, not a *notion* of what he did or stood for that led to his killing, by its nature dreadful because it is in cold blood. His death feels wholly arbitrary because no motive is supplied or suggested. In this film's eerie political emptiness, execution by firing squad becomes merely *ordinary*—a repetitious daily event like sunrise or the six o'clock news. In real life, the execution would have appeared unjust to some observers, and proper to others; it would have been a purposeful political act. The execution as presented occurs without purpose or meaning.

One soldier in the firing squad is tenderhearted and will not pull the trigger: Robert Cummings. For his compassion he will be sent to the front. He runs away and falls in love, and the plot of this falling-in-love is astonishing. It begins as we see two strangers parting, a man and a woman whom we have not met. We understand that they have just made love, and that she is a prostitute; they seem fond of each other, happy, making plans for their next encounter, and as the man walks into the street we spy his shape down the sight of a rifle—as a sniper shoots him dead. Although we must assume that the sniper waited for this particular man, no detail supports the assumption; we know nothing of this man or his killer or why anyone would want to kill him; we know nothing about the shooting except the fact. Like the execution, this street-killing—erotic idyll ended by bullet—presents itself as wholly random or arbitrary.

It is this young woman with whom Cummings falls in love— and she with him: immediately. After Mack and Cummings drag her dead lover's body into her flat, they talk; Cummings wants the dead man's pass for the last train. Soon enough, they scheme a double escape. During their brief courtship, these characters in their dialogue establish the farm-in-Valencia to which the train will deliver them—erecting the Arcadian alternative to Madrid. The dialogue is typically hackneyed. "This war can't go on forever," says Helen Mack as her lover stiffens in the adjacent room. (She has just said: "A moment ago he was so happy.") Toward the end of the film, as Mack and Cummings ride a wagon toward the train, it becomes her random turn to die. This time there is a hint of purpose; the killers want to hijack the wagon to get to the train themselves. However, it is arbitrary that

Mack is the one to die—unless, under another agenda, she dies because she is not a virgin. (She should die for her dialogue.) Cummings makes it to the train alone.

In fact, there are few deaths in *Last Train from Madrid*. Channelsurfing today's television, happening upon a Chuck Norris special, you will see more carnage before you can switch channels than you'll observe in eighty minutes of this film. I remembered one more death from 1937. While the train remains in the station—only people with passes admitted on board—guards move through the cars rechecking passes. As they demand papers from everyone, our anxiety mounts because they approach a vulnerable protagonist. Suddenly, looking at one man's pass—a stranger to us—the guards ask him to step outside. He looks nervous; he tries to run—and they shoot him down. They kill him *on purpose*, aiming their guns, yet they kill him *for no reason* that we understand.

Murderous paradox drives the film: Malignity exists everywhere, yet most of the time it appears motiveless. To the psyche, all these deaths are as arbitrary as death by bombs from the sky. One air raid takes its place at the center of the film, a riot of civilian panic, people running and frightened. The soundtrack plays fear music, camera shots are quick and angular, and in one quick shot nervous pigeons scurry.

In Robert Frost's "Design," he writes about the malign coincidence of an invisible spider haply arranged to kill a fly; the poet asks what could have caused this coming-together except for "design of darkness to appall." Then he qualifies the question in a further line: "If design govern in a thing so small." In

The Last Train from Madrid we are surrounded by fear of im-
minent death, but, horribly, we lack design. As humans we wish
or need to understand the cause or to place blame—on an enemy, on politicians who betrayed us, on the cupidity or moral
squalor of a person or a class of people—because blame implies
purpose, and it is our nature to wish to understand causes for our
misfortunes. We search for anything that we may hold responsible for our fate: God, our political leaders, the Devil, the
planets in conjunction at our births, the sins of our fathers, Muslims, biorhythms, Queen Elizabeth II, or a witch's curse. The
film suggests that design may not govern in a thing so small as
human life and death.

Print at the beginning of *Last Train from Madrid* scrolls its
neutrality; this movie will not uphold or defend either side of this
war. This neutrality becomes vacancy, motiveless horror. When
we read of battles in old histories, we study the motives of each
side although the cause may mean little to us. "The river ran red
with blood for seven days," we may remember—not, "Thus
Centerville retained its passage to the Danube"—but always we
understand that there appeared to be reasons for blood. By omit-
ting ideology, *Last Train* purifies war from its historical context
into pointless anonymous suffering. The film scrolls war's utter
panic and sorrow. Oh, sorrow, sorrow, sorrow—the ripe life cut
by hate without purpose, by anger lacking reason, by murder
without blame.

How did my mother happen to take an eight-year-old to such a
movie? Microfilm of the *New Haven Register* explains: The

newspaper printed paragraphs of studio puffery that wholly misrepresented the film: "With but two pictures to her credit, both of which were outstanding successes, Dorothy Lamour, the glamourous brunette, one of the season's most sensational 'finds,' moves into the ranks of the screen's charming leading ladies. The event takes place in 'The Last Train from Madrid,' the romance laid in war-torn Spain." I find it breathtaking to read this notice of the film that horrified me. "In this story Miss Lamour appears as a beautiful patrician girl, who is the beloved of a young lieutenant in the government forces and his best friend." When I read Frank S. Nugent's *New York Times* review (6/19/37) I am almost as astonished. He notes the lack of politics in this "glib little fiction" but for Nugent there was also no horror. "True, it speaks of the Spanish revolution, but merely as Hollywood has, in the past, regarded the melodramatic turmoils of Ruritania and Zenda." He calls the film "a pre-tested melodrama which should suit the average palate," and in his conclusion makes a joke: "Its sympathies, neither Loyalist nor Rebel, are clearly on the side of the Ruritanians."

Frank S. Nugent was not eight years old. Was Nugent's cynicism more appropriate than my horror? At eight, I ignored the silly romance at the film's center and registered only the panic of unmotivated murder. When I returned home after the Saturday matinee, I packed my lead toy soldiers with their flattish Great War helmets into a shoebox and tucked it deep in the long closet of my bedroom. I performed the ritual with so much solemnity that I might have played taps for background music. By this time I felt not panic but a sadness that would not relent, which may have derived from another melancholy that absorbed me that weekend. The film opened in New Haven on Saturday, July 10, 1937, while Amelia Earhart was missing over the Pacific. I remember playing outside the house, keeping the window open and a radio near the window; I remember a report that the Navy had spotted her plane on an atoll: I remember the correction of the report. In my mind's eye, Amelia Earhart circled continually, high in the air, the hum of the Lockheed's engine distant and plaintive, gas almost gone, the pilot in her leather helmet peering for land as she circled . . .

It must have been a month or two later, maybe a cool September day, that something on the radio or in a headline reminded me of the film. Spain and China were in the news. On that day, alone in the house, I carried my War Cards down cellar to the coal furnace. I was not allowed to open the furnace door but I opened it anyway and threw the War Cards onto the red coals. At first they smoldered and turned brown and I feared that they would not burn, would give me away when my father came home and fixed the furnace. Then one card burst into bright yellow flame, then another, then all together flared briefly in the shadow-and-red hellfire of the furnace on Ardmore Street.

AFTERWORD:
"WE HAVE LIVED
BY OUR WITS"

Poetry is what I care about the most. Once I did the annual "Education of a Poet" lecture, for the Academy of American Poets, telling stories about getting started. When they ask you to lecture, they call you "poet," so the presumption is not your own. Now, when I speak of my education as an essayist, I don't intend to compare myself to Michel de Montaigne. I make my living as a freelance writer, and most of these essays were magazine pieces undertaken to pay the grocer. If I had been born to a trust fund, how many would I have written?

Some of them. I write prose not only for money, but because paragraphs provide the best way to do some things—arguments, reminiscences—that I want to do. Prose came hard for me, and I have been stubborn about learning how to do it. At the end of this miscellaneous *Principal Products of Portugal*, I want to reminisce about studying—with the help of William Shawn and other teachers—the trade or art of the essay.

When I decided, at fourteen, that I would be a poet all my life, I knew that poetry would not supply a livelihood. In 1942 we did not know that poets would become college teachers by profession as they were once vicars or journalists. I decided in my ignorance that I would support myself by writing prose. One hundred years later, that's just what I do, but at fourteen, I assumed I would support myself by fiction. Consumed by the ardors and arduousness of verse, I saw myself turning out novels for rent money. When I was seventeen I wrote eighty thousand words called *The Loves of Hilary Smart*, a comic satiric portrait of the artist at fourteen. When Hilary succeeded at last in kissing his love on the cheek, he had the sniffles and apologized for dribbling a booger. One publisher wrote a benign note, affronting me with his condescension. Trying again at twenty I wrote a novel shorter and worse. Adamant in my preference for poetry, I proved my point by writing sloppy prose. At twenty-one I renounced fiction.

But if you devote yourself to poetry—writing it, reading it, judging it, arguing your enthusiasms and anathemas—you must write prose for poetry's sake. You *talk* about the art—sometimes it's called "criticism"—because you are passionate (both ways) about certain new poets. At Oxford I wrote the first essay I was paid for: "American Poets since the War" spread its bad sentences over the pages of a London monthly.

During two years in England I met grownup poets when they visited Oxford, and often discovered that they supported themselves by working for newspapers or the BBC. Louis MacNeice, W. R. Rogers, Henry Reed, and Dylan Thomas produced or wrote for radio. Other writers reviewed novels and biographies in the weeklies (*New Statesman*, *Listener*) and the

Sunday Times and *Observer*. They lived in the country, for the low overhead, and went up to London once a week to pick out books for reviewing. V. S. Pritchett supported his short stories by writing reviews, Edwin Muir his poetry. In Majorca, Robert Graves turned out novels, essays, casuals for *Punch*, crank anthropology, and memoirs—to make a living. I read Graves's poem in which he spoke proudly about his shelf of prose books, written in honest English—but said that he would not explain why he wrote them lest he seem foolish, like the man who spent his life raising dogs because he liked cats so much.

Despite these English freelance models, I became a professor. After living off fellowships for six years in my twenties, I took a job teaching literature. When I wrote prose, I wrote only about poetry. Doing an MLA paper on the idea of organic form, I tried university wit: "To flatter the Word, we call it flesh." When the *New York Times* asked me to review Wright Morris's book of essays, which I admired, I fell into Lecturer's Manner ("Perhaps, however, we are less pleased when Morris . . .") and the *Book Review* never printed it. I felt chagrin and exasperation at my failure. As a competitive sort, I was annoyed to think that there were ordinary literary tasks that I was not up to. Therefore I set out to learn to write a readable newspaper review. It took me several years and many failures, if I ever did learn.

There were things that I wanted to write about, more important to me than book reviews, that I could not accommodate to the poems I was writing. Paragraphs not lines would reconstitute the stories my grandfather told me, summers when we hayed together. Late in my twenties I began *String Too Short to Be Saved*, in order to preserve times, places, and people that I cherished, who would otherwise slip into oblivion; my paragraphs wanted to slow the journey down.

The first chapter of *String* took more than twenty drafts, the last chapters three. For every new literary undertaking, there seems to be an ur-sentence or stylistic template that suggests characteristic diction, tone, syntax, and rhythm. I cannot find this sentence by reasonable thought; I have to search for it as among papers on a desk. I may look for years; I may find it on the second page of a scratch pad. But I need to find it before I can write my essay or my book.

Once I have found it, I do not entirely lose it. When I write reminiscent prose thirty-five years after *String*, I start with the sentence I discovered then, altered through the years (in expansiveness or inclusion; in punctuation) the way people age and remain the same. A subject-style stores itself in the preconscious where we retain behavior like riding a bicycle, putting on a sweater, or writing iambic pentameter—procedures neither remembered nor forgotten. It took me several drafts to find the mode for *Dock Ellis in the Country of Baseball* (1976); ten years after I finished the book, I needed to find the style or tone again, to write a summary chapter for a reprint. As I started the new chapter, I felt new sentences glide along old pathways: I knew the tune of what was coming next.

After the first chapter of *String* took me twenty-odd drafts, the essay or story was (symmetrically) rejected by twenty-odd magazines. While I worked on succeeding chapters, melancholy notes arrived from my agent. First, the *New Yorker* sent "The Wild Heifers" back, having *quite* liked it; I was disappointed, because at that time the *New Yorker* published much memoir, sponsoring a bevy of soft sensuous memory books. After the *New Yorker*, the *Atlantic* turned it down, *Harper's*—and absolutely everybody else. The last rejection came from *Story*; they would have paid $40 had they liked it well enough.

Nevertheless, I kept on with the book. (It was not that I *expected* periodical publication.) One day, writing in England in a 1485 house—pre-Columbian!—I invented a lost railroad on Ragged Mountain where an abandoned locomotive rusted, grown over by bushes and young trees. My book was reminiscence and therefore nonfiction, as it were; but when I lied about the railroad, my pencil raced and my heart pounded: The invented ruin of a train embodied splendid loss and archaic remain. By telling lies I wrote the best pages of *String Too Short to Be Saved*—and learned something about fiction; and let myself in for a lifetime of New Hampshire teasing: "Been up to see that railroad of yours lately, Dawn?"

When I returned to the United States from the English year, I sent the manuscript to the Viking Press, which had published two books of my poems. They liked it and scheduled it for 1961.

Meantime, I had supported my family by my wits for a whole year. We had left Ann Arbor with two thousand dollars, for a year of writing in the Essex village of Thaxted, and returned with two thousand dollars. We lived in the large old Priory—two adults, a five-year-old, and a baby—with a coal furnace misleadingly called central. It took the chill off three or four of the ten rooms. In the kitchen there was a coke stove that heated the kitchen. Each morning I started a coal fire in the basket grate in the little room where I wrote poems. Afternoons, I made another coal fire in "the music room" on the second floor, big enough to hold everybody when it warmed up. I wrote much of *String* in the music room as the fire got going.

Also I wrote poetry reviews for the *New Statesman* for six months. I wrote for *Encounter*, and for a flat fee co-edited *A Concise Encyclopedia of English and American Poetry and Poets* with Stephen Spender. I interviewed Henry Moore for the American *Horizon*, a *Paris Review*–style interview. I tried purely commercial writing: In Ann Arbor a friend edited *Continental*, a Ford Motor Company publication addressed to purchasers of an expensive motorcar. "What do they want to read about?" I asked my friend. "Tell them ways to spend their money." Thus, I wrote about shopping for antiques in England—after interviewing dealers, visiting Sotheby's, and reading journals. Since I could not distinguish a Georgian breakfront from an espaliered yew tree I wrote the piece using nonsense in lieu of appropriate items, counting on my wife to substitute something probable. At the House of Spottiswood in Bath, I assured *Continental* drivers, you could purchase for a pittance a genuine balsawood seventeenth-century *abattoir* . . .

Mostly I worked for the BBC. For the Third Programme I read my poems, chose and introduced the poems of others, interviewed and was interviewed, made a script out of Williams's *Paterson*, acted in the production, and helped to direct it. For the Home Service I wrote brief talks to fill the intermissions of concerts, and for two four-week sessions I was book critic among *The Critics*, a popular program that played Sundays at noon. Around a table at Broadcasting House sat a book critic, an art critic, a theatre critic, a movie critic, a television and radio critic, and a chairperson. Each week I chose a book and wrote a three-minute review. After I read my comments, the other critics—who had also read the book—chimed in, as I chimed in about the art exhibition, play, movie, and radio or television show that the other critics assigned. *The Critics* replayed on Thursdays, we were paid twice, and it was lucrative work.

Toward the end of that happy year, my wife and I considered remaining in Thaxted. We loved the village life; I loved the freelance life. But to stay and make my living, I would need a work permit, notoriously difficult to acquire; nor was I ready to become an *English* poet. We returned to Ann Arbor and the University; but I promised my wife, before we left, that we would return after three years.

Viking began the process of publishing *String Too Short to Be Saved*. Meantime I taught classes and wrote poems. Because of my glimpse of the writing life, I also tried writing children's books and magazine pieces. Largely I failed: I wrote several wordy and inflated children's books; finally, *Andrew the Lion Farmer* was published with a good editor's help. I worked on an essay about the creative process, aiming at a general magazine like the *Atlantic*, and, after my agent flogged the article for a year, ended by selling it to a quarterly for ten cents. In Manhattan at a party I met the *Harper's* editor who had rejected it; he claimed to regret turning the essay down, but "an essay is like a sonnet." I had failed at essay-form.

Then, at Viking, the public relations department sent out bound galleys of *String* to solicit quotes. Pat MacManus had the intelligence to send a copy to E. B. White. He forwarded his galley to his stepson Roger Angell at the *New Yorker*, not yet baseball's Thucydides, and Angell wrote saying that the magazine wished to buy two chapters, including "The Wild Heifers," and that they wished they had known about these essays earlier; they would have printed more of them . . .

Viking delayed the book's publication by a month, to give the *New Yorker* time to print two pieces. (The other was "A Day on Ragged," called "The Blueberry Picking" in the book, where I invented the railroad.) Needless to say, I wrote Roger Angell that, as it happened, the *New Yorker* had indeed "known about these essays earlier;" they had rejected "The Wild Heifers" in 1959. When Roger answered, he had looked into the earlier rejection. Slight differences in taste or opinion, as Roger said, can account for a rejection here and an acceptance there; it *happens*, Roger told me, but please, he said, please, don't tell other writers about this.

Early in the 1960s I looked into another kind of writing. Annoyed at textbooks on writing, approached by a publisher who wanted a poetry anthology, I entered the zany universe of the textbook. (The aging textbook-guru, late at night on vodka, insists: "Glue a half dollar into the binding. Some night when they want a Pepsi, you've solved your used-book problem.") Anthologies I had done before, not as textbooks but as instruments of taste—reward for virtue, blame for vice. Now by means of textbooks I tried imposing my ideas about prose style, on the one hand; on the other, I collected old poems together to advance my pedagogical and literary notions. Now I looked to make a living as well as to impose ideas.

Another freelance Thaxted year approached, this time financed by a Guggenheim, and I looked forward to concentrated work. After my two *String* chapters appeared in his magazine, William Shawn of the *New Yorker* said he would like to speak with me when I visited New York. I was admitted to the presence, which was short, pink, soft, polite, mannered, kindly, and formal. Mr. Shawn rose to his full height, significantly above desktop, and greeted me with generous words about my prose. (They had done some poems for almost a decade.) Mr. Shawn would like to see more of it. Was I interested in moving to New York?

With two small children, with a good job, with a disinclination to become "a *New Yorker* writer," I said no; but a notion flipped into my head. When I last met Henry Moore, I told him I wanted to see more of him. Would it be all right, sometime, if I wrote an essay about him? He seemed pleased with the idea. Now I asked William Shawn, "Would you like a profile of Henry Moore?" Mr. Shawn excused himself, left the room, and returned a moment later to say, "Yes. Fine. Please do." I suppose he checked to see if another writer had dibs on Moore. Thus were three years laid out for me. I was too innocent to think about asking for expenses.

The next year in Thaxted, 1963–64, I wrote little poetry. It was an unhappy year, reverse of the visit three years before, although I worked for the BBC again and reviewed for English papers. I wrote a play about Robert Frost, documentary theatre that learned from Joan Littlewood. (Over two or three years, I fumbled through many drafts. During weekly journeys to New York, before it opened in 1965 with Will Geer at the Theatre de Lys, I rewrote in the green room while the cast rehearsed.) Mostly I worked on the Henry Moore piece. I visited Castleford in Yorkshire, the coal-mining town in Yorkshire where he was born, and talked with Moore's old friends. I talked with his cronies from art school days, with old assistants, with young artists who loved him and others who loathed him, with museum directors, dealers, art historians, critics, and figures of English art: Francis Bacon, Barbara Hepworth, Herbert Read, Sir Kenneth Clark. The name of the *New Yorker* opens doors. Clark had me to lunch at his castle in Kent, where Thomas à Beckett stayed on his way to and from France. Picking me up at the depot, Clark drove through greensward to the castle. "The rich in England," he remarked, "are still very rich."

Mostly I learned about Henry Moore from Henry Moore. We played ping-pong, drank tea and whiskey, talked and talked. I spent one whole day following him and watching him work. (In this book "Henry Moore's Day"—adapted from the opening of the profile—preserves that December day in 1963.) Later that month, I asked Moore if I could buy a drawing. I would have preferred sculpture but I thought I might afford a drawing. I knew that Henry sold things to his friends on easy terms, over periods as long as ten years. "We'll see," said Henry, looking agreeable but preoccupied. Late in the day, he told me that his stock of drawings was *low*; would I mind a bronze maquette instead? He led me to a storeroom over the old living room at Hoglands where he kept families of small models, or sketches for bigger pieces: beautiful things. I chose a maquette of the alternative to the Lincoln Center piece, a two-part reclining figure. "Good choice," said Henry. "That's my favorite."

I was petrified: "What will it cost?" I asked. Henry said, "That's your Christmas box."

After eight or ten months of interviewing, researching, taking notes, sorting and assorting, I was ready to begin writing. But I wasn't ready to begin writing because I didn't have any notion how to do a profile. I clobbered together a draft, sloppily arranged by category or topic mixed with chronology . . . It was no good and I knew it but I didn't know why. I did another draft, and another: The sentences became literate but the whole was slack, fuzzy, confusing, unfocused, and unreadable.

Many times in writing I have been certain that a piece was wrong yet had no notion what to do about it. At such a time I need outside help, a friend's or an editor's. Many times a good reader—professional or not, working over poems, essays, magazine articles, plays, children's books—has told me what was wrong, allowing me to revise. Sometimes I have submitted a commissioned manuscript with a cry for help, and received it. Not always. Once I finished a textbook, certain that it wasn't right. Sending it to the publisher, I apologized and asked for advice. I heard nothing, until a note arrived giving me dates for copy-edit and proof. Wait a minute, I wrote; what's *wrong* with it? A letter came back, signed by a vice president: "We have decided to have someone read your book."

Of course, sometimes I have thought that things were wrong when they were right. Although I felt sure that the Moore piece was bad, I didn't *know* that it was. I sent the completed or abandoned manuscript to the *New Yorker* and the Viking Press. After a month Viking turned the book down. I waited on the *New Yorker* another month, and another; then came the *New Yorker*'s rejection, four or five narrow lines from Mr. Shawn: "We are sorry that . . ." It was a sharp knife—no reason given, no suggestions—that cut cleanly.

It seemed hopeless, a wasted project. But by coincidence, a letter arrived just then from an editor at Harper Bros., expressing interest in my work, possibly in adding me to the Harper list. Of course I sent them the Henry Moore manuscript; they took it on, not without misgiving: It needed *work*, they said—maybe a lot of work. Would I come to New York soon? I came to New York soon, to have lunch with the Harper editor Jack Leggett and discuss revision. My agent suggested that, since I was in New York, I should phone the *New Yorker* to speak with Mr. Shawn. I did and he politely asked me to drop by—but let me know that I should hold no hope for the Moore as a *New Yorker* profile.

At lunch, Jack Leggett came up with a notion for construction. My present manuscript was an organizational mishmash—by topic (modeling and carving) and chronology (a job; a show; reviews; a holiday in France) and personal themes (reclining figures, family groups.) Leggett suggested that I construct each chapter around one work of art that exemplified its period.

As I entered Shawn's office, stacked high with manuscript, he was scrupulous again to hold no hope for the profile. Then, over an hour of talk, he told me what was wrong. The manuscript had flown back to my agent three months earlier, yet Shawn quoted sentences word-for-word. If I worried that his curt rejection meant cursory judgment, I worried no longer. When I left his office I looked for a place to sit down and make notes, but there were no chairs in *New Yorker* hallways. I sat on the floor and wrote Shawn's ten commandments of factual or objective prose. Thirty years later, I cannot find the list. Gently but decisively Shawn let me know that I had explained things to the reader when I didn't have to. I told about playing ping-pong with Moore: If he couldn't use his backhand, he hit the ball with the palm of his left hand, saying, "That *counts*, doesn't it?" I like the story—but when I told it in my draft of a profile, I kindly informed the reader that the story illustrated Moore's competitiveness. Not only did I explain the self-explanatory; in my zeal, I would not allow readers to make their own judgments. I praised the obviously praiseworthy and flattered the ordinary. By way of illustration, Shawn quoted from a hagiographic biography of a painter in which the author said things like, " 'Please pass the salt,' he said, wittily."

And I used other devices to block Moore from the reader. I told how Moore flew to Holland with his friend the writer Constantine Fitzgibbon, saying more or less: "Constantine Fitzgibbon tells how he and Henry took a taxi from the airport"—useless detail from an interview, blah blah blah—"and at the museum Moore walked briskly past Vermeers and"—a dozen esteemed Dutch and Flemish painters—"to stand for forty minutes looking at Rembrandt's 'Night Watch' while Fitzgibbon vainly tried to engage him in conversation." Out of mistaken obligation to give credit to my informer—or out of the interviewer's fatal wish to use *every* note he takes—I set between Moore and the reader the bulk of Moore's substantial but irrelevant friend. The cure for this disease was easy: Show Moore alone, doing what he did, head-on.

Most of Shawn's diagnosis of my invalid prose made immediate sense to me. With the shape or sequence supplied by Jack Leggett, with Shawn's implied unobserved observer, I felt that I could fly home and write the book. I flew home and wrote the book, or at least the first chapter about Moore's day. After two or three quick drafts, I mailed the chapter to Shawn. Almost immediately the phone rang: If the profile continued as it started, Mr. Shawn wanted it. It did, he did—and the tutelage of William Shawn allowed me to learn another kind of prose.

When the *New Yorker* bought the profile, my experience of Mr. Shawn had not concluded. Galley proof arrived with a hundred and fifty queries a page. The first alteration proposed by the editorial hand—I'm not sure how much Shawn did at this point—expressed classic *New Yorker* fact-fetishism, answering the ectoplasmic marginal "Who he?" of Harold Ross. My first sentence had been, "Henry Moore gets up at seven-thirty." (I like to begin a long piece with a blurt-sentence.) In galley the sentence was amended: "Henry Moore, the English sculptor, gets up at seven-thirty." Those commas softened my blurt but I knew enough not to challenge Ross's ghost.

Otherwise, the first galleys removed my commas and replaced them with *New Yorker* commas (and apologies); my thats became whiches, and my whiches thats. Most queries were factual, and most asked for *more facts*. It wasn't enough to claim that an exhibition opened in July of 1933; what *day* in July? Which *side* of Leicester Square? Then, someone felt that one sentence needed another adjective. Moore had built a bronze foundry in his back yard (before I was around) so that he could understand the founding process by doing it himself. Henry told me that he built the forge of stone; the *New Yorker* needed to know what *color* the stone was. When I could not tell them, they telephoned Moore in Hertfordshire.

With page proof, a week after galley, the number of queries dropped to fifty or sixty a column, still concerned largely with commas and house-style correctness. Goodness knows, I was grateful to be corrected, when I mistakenly substituted the *Spectator* for the *New Statesman* or *rugby* for *soccer*. In those days, only the *New Yorker* had a checking department, and only the *New Yorker* consulted writers before rewriting them. The *New Yorker* appeared to *like* writers. The old *Atlantic* once omitted two late paragraphs from an essay I wrote, as I discovered when I read the issue. (Two decades later, after a former *New Yorker* editor took over, the new *Atlantic* telephoned London to ask my permission for cuts in another essay.) The *New York Times Book Review*, the old *Tribune*, the *Saturday Review of Literature*, *Es-*

quire—regularly revised and cut a writer's language with a fine disregard for the devices and desires of a writer's heart. If sometimes the *New Yorker*'s checking department seemed a little dense, especially when they questioned the facts of poems, I was grateful.

The final round of questioning came directly from the editor. As the issue went to bed a week before publication, the telephone rang at 6:00 P.M.—the piece was a two-parter; this happened twice—and I heard Mr. Shawn's gentle voice: "Ah, Mr. Hall, and how are you today?" "Fine, Mr. Shawn, and how are you?" "Quite well, Mr. Hall. Several of us have gone through your profile, Mr. Hall, and I have a number of questions." "Go right ahead, Mr. Shawn." "There are *quite* a few, Mr. Hall. I think it may take us several hours." Weakly: "Go right ahead, Mr. Shawn." "In the first paragraph we have found a serial comma we think we might with profit remove." *Very* weakly: "Go right ahead, Mr. Shawn."

After the appearance of the Henry Moore piece, my private life continued to disintegrate, and for a time I wrote little. The sap drained from poetry's tree, and what I wrote was third-rate. With a divorce in the works, I struggled to make a textbook for a large advance. I did another *New Yorker* profile, of Eugene Power, who founded University Microfilms in Ann Arbor, which the *New Yorker* paid for and never printed. Disheartening: I had let my subject down; I could not find the sentence to make the technology as surprising as it was, much less to embody the fervor that my entrepreneur brought to his ideas. In the 1970s I talked with Shawn about other prose pieces, but I never committed myself to them.

After five years of the single life, I remarried in 1972, and in 1975 left my job teaching and moved to New Hampshire with Jane Kenyon to freelance. (There are two freelancers in this house; Jane has published four books of poems, a pamphlet of translations, and many essays.) I had children in college and terror in my heart. The textbook on prose style, *Writing Well*, supplied a base income. I set to expanding my writing for magazines. I did a piece about baseball in *Playboy*. (Roger Angell properly owned the *New Yorker* franchise.) Everybody writes best out of obsession, or love, and I loved this old game. I could never have made the big leagues as an athlete, but as a writer I could spend an hour in a dugout with Pete Rose and drink orange blossoms with Wilver Stargell. Writing about Dock Ellis, I found entry to a black country I had never visited.

Now I wrote for *Esquire*, *Ford Times*, *Yankee*, *Sports Illustrated*, *Architectural Digest*, and *Harper's*. When I found a new enthusiasm I wrote out of it—as when I installed a satellite dish and sunbathed in an abundance of baseball and basketball. My longest passion has been the place I live in, which I first visited (I am told) when I was six weeks old. I have written much about Eagle Pond and New Hampshire. The Hood Museum at Dartmouth asked for an essay on winter, for the catalog of a cold exhibition. *Harper's* reprinted that essay, a joy to write, which I followed with three companion pieces, collected in *Seasons at Eagle Pond*. Over the years I collected essays into books by topic—on sport, on New Hampshire, on poetry. When the

phone rang from an editor, I thought: If I do this piece, can I
collect it into a book? One secret of freelancing is to sell everything as many times as you can. Another is to listen. My cousin
Paul Fenton told me the story of the oxcart man, which became
a poem, a children's book, and a paragraph in an essay. At store,
post office, and church, I keep my eyes and ears open.

This is the way we live now: A freelancer's income, as I note
every year when I do my income tax, derives from the thousand
things: a little editing, many poetry readings, book reviews, lectures, royalties on two dozen books in print, advances on forthcoming books—and sales to magazines. Often editors telephone asking me to repeat myself: If I write a piece looking into
the literary interest in baseball, an editor soon calls to ask if I
will investigate the literary interest in baseball. On the other
hand, I repeat myself on purpose, returning to a topic because I
have not exhausted it, or because I have a new idea. Writing both
poetry and prose, fiction and nonfiction and even drama, I approach the same material from two (or seven) points of style and
view. No one blames Cezanne for returning to the same rocks
and the same townscape. I claim a writer may do a scene again
from another angle, in a different season, with new light at another time of day.

Often I struggle to write something that looked easy until I
tried. My piece about Carlton Fisk took twenty-nine drafts, I
have no idea why. Other essays finish in four or five tries, but
most take something like nine or ten. Usually, it is a new subject
or a new audience that makes an essay difficult. Sometimes I

immerse myself in a magazine that's new to me, trying to intuit the ear to which my sentences must address themselves. Doing a book, gradually I discover myself imagining the person to whom I speak—but not on purpose; I find the addressed ear in the process of writing. The sense of one reader—as when, talking into a microphone for radio, you speak to a single listener driving a car—makes for consistency in tone, vocabulary, syntax; it makes for boundaries of knowledge and sensibility. Doing a picture book for five-year-olds, you do not use the vocabulary or syntax you address to readers of the *Iowa Review* or the *TLS*. Or if you do, you had better look for another line of work.

Writing for many years, a freelancer uses many voices. When I read over past work, as when I look through old essays for this collection, I am shocked by the manyness of the author. "Is this supposed to be one person?" I fear that I am a chameleon or a hypocrite, talking one way for *Yankee*'s audience and another way for the readers of *Harper's*. "Is the admirer of Red Auerbach and Henry Adams, of Ted Williams and E. A. Robinson, the same fellow?"

Sure. I think of an old friend who said of herself, "I'm not a person; I'm a boarding house." Picasso claimed that every human being was a colony. Freelance writers learn to speak from time to time out of a large internal cast of characters.

Writing poems first and prose second, I meditate continually about the relationship between the devices. My poetry and my prose, as I believe, help each other out, sometimes doing "the same thing" in opposite ways: the one way loose and multiple

in detail; the other tight, narrow, and intense. Emerson sometimes approached topics first in his journals, discursive and in-
conclusive, then gathered similar material into the loose bag of
a lecture, then cut and organized it into an essay, then made a
poem as a final distillation. When I write prose I can *include*: I
can elaborate examples and tell an anecdote or follow a speculation; I can digress, argue, describe . . . Although my poems
have become more inclusive in later years, still they seek intensity by diminishing qualification and reducing detail.

Certainly my poetry is harsher than my prose. Art is the product of many conflicts resolved into one object: many and one;
unity and diversity; form and energy; rhyme and reason; sweetness and harshness. The further one goes in one direction, the
further one may—or must—go in the other. The beauty or sensuousness of poetry infuses the body with delicious sound, image, and metaphor. Prose does similar things but with less in-
sistent concentration. Because poetry delights the senses more,
it can accommodate—for its ultimate power and beauty—
darker embodiments of loss and devastation. Because readers
enjoy the beautiful devastation of poetry's pulse and thunder,
they welcome its intense harsh conflicted joy.

The process of writing prose *resembles* the process of writing poetry, as it must do, in its reliance on swings of mood, but
as usual prose swings not so intensely. Always, bipolarity provides the rhythm—supplying and denying, writing and crossing
out and writing again. All humans are bipolar and writers are
extreme; most writers suffer from bipolar mood disorder, or
manic-depressive disease, largely without delusion but with

painful depression and the elated energy of mania. My own bipolarity is subclinical; I tend toward mild mania, a cheerful fellow interrupted by long mild depressions. But even within a day, there may be frequent changes. My writing, prose and poetry, makes use of the surge that supplies or bestows (without judgment) and equally makes use of mania's dour twin, the skeptical critical denial that sees through, finds fault, and crosses out. The process of writing requires combined opposite moods as art requires unity and variety, repetition and change.

The life of freelance writing is an economics of thrust and repulse, with the goal of making art—breeding cats for the love of dogs—and staying alive. There is also the thrill and conceit of doing it oneself, of self-support by shrewdness like the entrepreneur's and the con man's. I feel as if I flew the Jolly Roger, and remember the excitement with which I heard Willa Muir answer my question about how she and Edwin had supported themselves over the decades. (Do I repeat myself? Therefore I repeat myself.) Her answer was proud but it was neither a pride of literature nor an assertion of the work's value. It did not gainsay prizes, fellowships, or sinecure; it did not deny the help of editors and friends. She drew herself up with triumph in getting by as she told me, "We have lived by our wits."

In gathering *Principal Products of Portugal*, I've returned to old paragraphs and worked them over; I've removed some repetition, remade some phrases, and added information—where time's passage has required it; I've named the circumstances of some interviews and altered tenses: It will no longer do to assert that "Henry Moore gets up at seven-thirty," unless I pretend to an awful knowledge.

When I ended *Life Work*, I said, "There is only one long-term project." This book—collecting and revising essays, writing new ones—is a short-term project. While I put these prose pieces together, I've been obsessed not with my own health but with my wife's. Yet every day, at home or beside her hospital bed, I do a little of what I have always done. Fretted by anxiety and dread, I take comfort for a few hours a day in resuming old habits; I take sentences apart and put them together again.